Secrets of Stoicism

Discover the Stoic Philosophy and the Art of Happiness; Increase Your Emotions and Everyday Modern Life by Following This Beginners Guide Suited for Entrepreneurs!

Pamela Hughes

Table of Contents

Table of Contents
Introduction
Chapter 1: History of Stoicism
Chapter 2: Background of Stoicism
Chapter 3: First Two Topoi

    Logic
    Physics

Chapter 4: The Third Topos (Ethics)
Chapter 5: Apatheia and the Stoic Treatment of Emotions
Chapter 6: Stoicism after the Hellenistic Era
Chapter 7: Contemporary Stoicism
Chapter 8: Stoics Spiritual Exercises
Chapter 9: Stoicism Is Ideal for the Real World
Chapter 10: Manage Your Emotions to Find Inner Peace
Chapter 11: Ways to Manage Anger Using Stoicism
Chapter 12: Understanding How and Why Anger Rises
Chapter 13: Stoic Philosophy and Anger
Chapter 14: Stoicism Reveals Rituals That Will Make You Confident
Chapter 15: Stoic Philosophy Ancient Wisdom in the Modern World
Chapter 16: The Four Cardinal Virtues
Chapter 17: Incorporation of Stoic Philosophy into Everyday Life

    How to Practice Stoicism

Chapter 18: Growing Up Stoic (Philosophical Education for Character, Persistence, and Grit)
Conclusion

Introduction

Many thanks for choosing us to share our knowledge with you on Stoicism. If Stoicism were a tree, we would cut it down, use its roots and leaves to make medicine, its branches to make beautiful benches to sit on while we enjoy its fruits. Thank God it is not, lest we be accused of deforestation but all the same we promise to share this "tree" with you. The goal of this book is to leave you with an underlying knowledge of Stoicism, how it helped people in ancient times, and how it can help you in today's world.

In this book, we will cover the following:
- The history of Stoicism
- The backgrounds of Stoicism
- The first two topos; logic and physics
- The third topos; ethics
- Apatheia and the stoic treatment of emotions
- Stoics after the Hellenistic era
- Contemporary Stoicism

Stoicism is a way of life that inclined people to act modestly and be of good character. As a reward, they were blessed with not only fortune and wealth but also happiness. With that said, I am hoping that by the time you complete this book, you will have decided on whether Stoicism is the right way of life or not. This book should open your eyes to whether Stoicism is a sham, or it is a philosophy that still works in modern society. Tighten your seat belts as we are about to embark on a long 'statistic journey' as we are not planning on leaving any stone unturned.

Chapter 1: History of Stoicism

Stoicism is a philosophy that enables people to exist in the best possible manner. It is used to help people lessen negative emotions, increase the positive ones, and help them polish their intrinsic worth. Stoicism provides practical ways to harvest more only from what was necessary. Stoicism is not complicated, and in its simplicity, it paves the way for practical ways to find serenity and advance a person's positive attributes.

Stoicism comes from prehistoric Greece and Rome at the beginning of the 3rd century B.C. Back then, people thought differently from the people of today. Their primary concern was avoiding poverty, and this made them behave, think, and make decisions geared towards preventing that. It is of great essence to note that they were aware that avoiding poverty was not a ticket to happiness. Despite their primary goal being to avoid poverty, they also aimed at an understanding of ways to have a brilliant soul. Stoicism became famous because it gave answers to fear, anxiety, and stress. It also provided solutions to day to day trials.

This philosophy encouraged good behaviors to get better life experiences. People worked towards having good behaviors for a reward of a better life and avoid negative behavior as the pay for that was a challenging life with problems. In summary, Stoicism was an ancient way of life that taught people how to live in a particular way. It focused on having good behaviors to reduce negativity and increase contentment. This philosophy has been tried and tested by famous philosophers like Tom Brady, Thomas Jefferson, George Washington, and many others. Stoicism might have started a long time ago, but it is as relevant today as it was then. What was the goal of Stoicism? It was created to be simple to understand, easy to act on it and be useful in our lives.

The stoics were a group of philosophers who formed the Stoic philosophy. Let us look at some of the stoics that contributed to this great philosophy.

- **Marcus Aurelius**

Now, Marcus was one remarkable and most influential person in the history of human beings. For two decades, he was the head of the Roman Empire. It was during his reign that Rome was the most civilized part of the world. Did I mention that he was a remarkable human being? Of course, history has recorded overtime on how Marcus never abused his power but instead lived the Stoic way of life. His writings on how he struggled to live as an honorable human being were discovered and published as Meditations. His writings made him the best example of how Stoicism helps people to deal with day to day stresses. Marcus Aurelius lived the stoic life as one good and wise human being.

- **Lucius Annaeus Seneca**

Lucius was a dramatist, writer, and statesman. His careers gave him a good grasp of words and real charisma. He explained Stoicism and memorably. His writings are the best start for anybody to begin the journey of philosophy. His thoughts easily resonate with the modern world of today because of the practical examples given on altruism, friendship, mortality, and time management.

Chapter 2: Background of Stoicism

Today's scholars only recognize three phases of Stoicism the early Stoa, the middle Stoa, and late Stoa. Of course, Stoicism was also a modification of the former schools of thought. Its influence was extensive even after the closure of philosophical schools in 529 C.E. by the Emperor of Byzantine Emperor Justinian I.

Philosophical Antecedents

Stoicism, being a Hellenistic eudaimonic, gets its influence from the former schools of thought, but at the same, it is openly critical to some of their ideology. The schools of thoughts that preceded Stoicism are:

- Aristotelianism
- Platonism
- Cynicism
- Skepticism
- Epicureanism

Eudaimonia was a word that represented happiness and flourishing. To the Greco-Romans, eudaimonia often represented good moral virtues. Stoicism stood out because of its different context from some school of thoughts of that time with the same ideology. For instance, Euthydemus, states there are only four good virtues, and everything else is neither bad nor good. According to McBrayer, the attributes are courage, temperance, justice, and wisdom. To Aristotle, the virtues were twelve, and all were important but not adequate for eudaimonia. Aristotle also explained that both effort and luck contribute significantly to a flourishing life.

The most significant contrast is seen in Cynics, where he agreed with Socrates that the only good was a virtue but disagreed with Aristotle's additions terming them as distractions. Cynics preached a simple life that is challenging to practice. They stated that virtue was the only good and that things like education, health, or wealth may or may not be preferred. Aristotelians, on the other hand, preached aristocratic, which explained that eudaimonia could not be achieved without some privileges.

Greek Stoicism

Exponents of Stoicism came from the Eastern Mediterranean. Stoicism was Socratic, and even the Stoics accepted that label. Zeno got his information from Cynic Crates, Epictetus writings, and his teachers Stilpo and Polemo. Zeno established the three topoi logic, physics, and ethics. Zeno of Tarsus and Diogenes of Babylon were the principal heads of Stoa for a long time, even though their contributions were not significant.

In 155 B.C., three heads of Athens' significant schools went to Rome for diplomatic reasons. The Roman public loved their public performances, and at the same time, they rubbed one Roman elite the wrong way, and this bore tension between politicians and philosophers. Between late II Century B.C.E. and early I Century B.C.E., Stoics renewed their liaison with the Academy. Poisonous and Panaetius sought an agreement among the Stoicism, Academicism, and Aristotelianism. This move brought Stoicism success.

Roman Stoicism

Between 88 and 86 B.C.E, Athenian, Peripatetic, and Epicurean Ariston led politics in Athens. In 92 B.C.E, Rome defeated Mithridates, and since Athens was in support of them, it was also defeated. It made philosophers escape to different places in the Mediterranean. Stoics emulated Cato the Younger because of his opposition to Julius Caesar. In the late First Century, Arius and Tarsus were the Stoic figures. In the Imperial period, the most excellent Stoics were Epictetus, Musonius Rufus, and Marcus Aurelius.

Between the Late Republic and the Empire, we get Stoicism from some sources like Cicero's books and Diogenes Laertius' literature. Some Stoics were persecuted through murder or exile during the reigns of Vespasian, Nero, and Domitian. Seneca committed suicide following Nero's orders, and Epictetus exiled. According to Gill, Epictetus was strict while Marcus was open.

Debate with other Hellenistic School

Hellenistic school of philosophy evolved because of dialogue among the philosophers. The dialogue brought about revision or adoption of new ideologies from other schools. The discussion was between Epicureanism, Platonism, Cynicism, Aristotelianism, and Epicureanism. Let us look at some examples to see how revision and adoption contributed to this evolution. Epictetus disagreed with Epicureans on their concern with pain and pleasure. For instance, Discourses 1.2.3 are all against Epicurus. Epictetus even suggests that Epicurus is confused and advises him to retire. Epictetus also attacked Skeptics by telling them that they keep proving themselves wrong every day, and they never give up. All the same, not all Stoics were against Epicurean and Academic.

Cicero hinted on the disagreement between Aristotelians and Stoics in his book De Finibus. We also have documented examples of change of Stoic's opinion because of being challenged by other schools. A good example is when Philopator adopted the determinism modified position because of criticism from Peripatetic. Stoic ideas were also included by other schools like Antiochus of Ascalon, who claimed that Zeno's ideas were embedded in Plato. We should also note that Stoicism evolved in Christianity through Middle Platonism.

Chapter 3: First Two Topoi

Logic

An essential part of Stoic philosophy is the two topics. It shows that ethic at the center and supported by physics and logic. Ethics, physics, and logic form Stoicism three topoi. Let us take a closer look at the logic as our first topoi.

There were early contributions by the Stoic on logic, and we have writings to support that. Stoics stated that their ideal figure Sage could attain faultless knowledge but relied on moral and cognitive progress in practice. It was because physics and logic are related to ethics and works in for its service. This idea was called "prokope," and it brought a dispute with Academic Skeptics. Stoics did not state that all parody was really like the Epicureans. They agreed that some were 'cataleptic' while others were not. Diogenes explained the differences better in VII.46. He stated that cataleptic comes from something existing while non-cataleptic comes from not living.

Stoics agreed that someone could have a wrong perception either in the form of a dream or hallucinations but at the same time, stated that with proper training, someone could distinguish cataleptic from non-cataleptic. Chrysippus said that impressions are essential to absorb because by doing so, we accumulate ideas that help us to form concepts and to make progress. We should note that cataleptic is not moderate knowledge. The Stoics impression was among apprehension, opinion, and education. An ascent of a cataleptic impact brings experience. Stoics supported a justification view and hence, one theory of truth like O'Connor.

Hankinson commented on the Academic Skeptics and Stoics dispute. Here, we find Stoic growth because of external pressure. Cicero lets us know that Zeno knew that an impression could come out of something existing and non-existing. It might not have solved the dispute, but it enhanced Stoic's growth on its impression that there can never exist two or more things that are precisely similar. Frede also brought growth to this view that the cataleptic impression becomes clear not because of any internal feature but because of the external elements. According to Frede, then Stoic is more "externalist" than "internalist." Skeptics' criticism showed evidence that they relied on knowledge (Goldman 94).

Athenaeus gives a story on Sphaerus, who was a student and colleague to Cleanthes and Chrysippus, respectively. He was shown a banquet of wax birds and was accused of giving assent to fake impressions when he tried to pick one. Sphaerus was clever, and he replied that he gave permission to the proposition of the thought of them being real but not to the actual claim that they were real birds. Stoic logic distinguished between "assertibles" and "sayables." "Sayables" are imperatives, questions oaths, curses, invocations, and also include "assertible." "Assertibles," on the other hand, are "sayables" that help us to make statements. The difference between Fregean propositions and Stoic's "assertibles" is that time can bring change to the truth or deception of "assertibles." Stoic's concerns were on their argument's validity and not on logic and truth. They also used logic to guard ethics and introduced modality to that logic.

Physics

This topoi encompasses metaphysics, theology, and the natural science of today's world. We will take a look at each one of them individually.

When it comes to metaphysically, they were determinists. According to Cicero, even if circumstances surrounding two events are similar, it is not a must that the results are similar, but they can be in the future even with the same factors to consider. Stoics did not include a chance in their concept, but that does not mean they did not think of it. No, they found it as a determinant of ignorance, and just like in today's world, events are simply events, and we don't know their causes. In theology, Stoics believed that there were living and non-living things. They recognized living things, including soul and God, and non-living things like void and time. It might contradict their stand on materialism, but to be fair, it is almost similar to modern philosophists who agree that one can talk of the abstract concept because we are the only ones who can judge ourselves physically.

They sought to understand nature through two principles; active and passive principles: logos, the active one, and the passive one that consists of substance and matter. The active principle cannot be generated and cannot be destroyed while the passive principle in the form of air, water, fire, and earth can be destroyed and created again. According to Stoics, cosmic conflagrations replicate themselves the same way because of nature and cannot change. It shows that the Stoics were not aware of God out of time and space because they reasoned that something spiritual could not take action on things, because it has no underlying powers. From all of that, White explains that it brings about a biological instead of a mechanical picture of the cause. It is considerably different from philosophies after Cartesian and Newtonian philosophy.

Some modern models also show varied or identical universe but do away with providence. Eusebius was quoted by White, stating that fire is like a seed that holds the principle of all substances causes of past, present, and future occurrences. Cicero explains the Stoic theory in De Fato by equating fate to the predecessor causes. Chrypissus also argued that there is never a movement without reason and relates that there is a cause for everything. This concept made Stoics embrace divination, not a false notion but as a subdivision of physic. Stoics accepted that for a person to predict the future, you don't ignore the laws, but you exploit them.

For cosmology and natural science, human beings should understand nature and allow it to assist us in having a eudaimonic life. For fundamental ontology, Stoics explained that atoms debased the concept of their seamless unity. The effects of physics on ethics are apparent, and Cicero summarizes them when he says that Chrysippus focused on the middle position in what we can view as a position between libertarianism and incompatibilism in the modern world. White and Spinoza took the weight away from honorable responsibility to dignity and self-worth.

Chapter 4: The Third Topos (Ethics)

This third topoi was a practical one. Ethics being the study of how people live their lives, was not easy. Early Stoics had a theoretical approach. Cleanthes, Zeno, and Chrysippus systematized and defended their doctrines from critics from Academics skeptics and Epicureans. They conceived the human nature as a social animal that would bring justice to people in regards to the way they lived — oikeiosis, which was a Stoic concept also related to this idea. For stoics, human beings have instincts that can be significantly advanced as we grow from childhood to adulthood — Stoics associated these instincts to justice, courage, temperance, and practical wisdom. We pursue goals using courage and temperance, justice is an extension for the concern on the increase of people in the world, and practical wisdom gives us knowledge on how to handle what we encounter in life.

Stoics accepted the four virtues and added more in each category. A good example is practical wisdom also included discretion and good judgment. Temperance carried self-honor, dignity, and self-control. Courage consisted of confidence, perseverance, and magnanimity. Justice, on the other hand, was associated with piety, sociability, and kindness. Chrysippus also explained the pluralism idea, and this unified the virtues more and made them inseparable. Haddot drew a different parallel between the virtues, the topois and Stoic discipline, which consist of action, assent, and desire. Desire or Stoic acceptance consists of teaching yourself to accept only the things found in the universe and nothing beyond that. Work, which is Stoic philanthropy, consists of human beings who should train themselves to be concerned by others in exercising justice. The discipline of assent, also known as Stoic mindfulness consists of human beings should know how to make decisions on what to reject and accept in this life by making a proper judgment.

Ethics tries to balance between elitists' view and asceticism. It elaborated on Stoics' view on dispreferred and preferred, as explained in the book on ethics by Zeno. Zeno taught the difference in things with value and without value. The first group consisted of health, education, and wealth, while the second one consisted of poverty, sickness, and ignorance. This move was a good one, and it enabled them to harvest from both the Peripatetic and Cynics. The connection between ethics and physics is that studying physics influences our understanding of ethics. Gregory Vlatos argued that 'theocratic' affects our concept of the relation between the order of cosmos and virtue. It is brought about by physics informing ethics through underdetermined fashion. Ethics is also not free from physics, as it can be understood directly through it. Many Stoics support Vlatos position, but some do not have a clear stand on the matter.

On the same ground, it would be fair to state that ancient stoic believed there was a god that was represented by the rational principle that arranged the cosmos and that distributed throughout the world in a manner that can be described as Pantheistic. We can also argue that Stoic metaphysics leave room for Atom or God, which they developed after being criticized by Epicureans.

Chapter 5: Apatheia and the Stoic Treatment of Emotions

In this chapter, we will focus on the differences between the Epicureans and Stoics. Epicureans' points out the different places that Stoas differs from Garden; he tells Lucilius, who is his friend, that he has no problem in borrowing ideologies from Epicurus as long as he sees sense in it. He tells him that he crosses the border as a spy and not as a deserter. As we had stated earlier, Stoics thought that the essential thing in this life is virtue, while Epicureans felt that it was to live moderately and avoid pain. All the same, eudaimonia was something that both schools upheld, and it was similar to both. To Stoics, it was apatheia, while to Epicureans, it was ataraxia. It was, however, evident that there were some differences in the two concepts, especially in how people would achieve the different states.

According to Epictetus, apatheia is liberty from passion, and ataraxia is tranquility. It is good to elaborate that 'passion' did not mean what we know in the current world. Today passion is all about emotions, but according to Stoics, passion was divided into healthy and unhealthy. In unhealthy, it consisted of fear, pleasure, pain, craving while in unhealthy, there was a delight, willing, discretion. It is good to note that pain did not have a corresponding positive item. To Stoics, passion is not emotions and instinctive reactions but consequences of judgment and asserting something. Stoics knew that there were reactions that we cannot control and, for that reason, focused on responses that we can control.

To Stoics, pain is not the hurt we feel, but the act of not avoiding something we know is terrible. Fear is expecting something terrible to happen; craving is the act of wanting something we term as good; pleasure is the act of choosing something not worth. On the other hand, eupatheiai is brought about by avoiding bad things, a good desire for willingness, and happiness over delight. All these are the reasons apatheia equates us in our experiences from what life throws at us: if we reason in those experiences, we will not care about the things that do not warrant our concern and be happy in the things that concern us.

Another difference between the two schools of thought is the route they take to get to apatheia and ataraxia. To Epicureans, ataraxia was an achievement that was obtained by avoiding pain and keeping away from political and social life. Epicurus sought close friendships but avoided extending their interactions further to avoid experiencing physical and mental pain. Stoic had a goal of exercising virtue, and this made them social beings. Marcus Aurelius insistently stated in Meditations that we need to wake up every day in the morning to be useful in our societies. Hierocles explained further cosmopolitism concept. It told how human beings should follow nature and be social while still making rational judgments. We can conclusively say that apatheia was not a Stoic's goal but a fruit of having a virtuous life.

Chapter 6: Stoicism after the Hellenistic Era

Stoicism has had an enormous influence in the modern world on Western philosophy; As Long listed the philosophers affected by Stoicism as Kant, Adam Smith, Descartes, Thomas More, Rousseau, Leibniz, and Augustine. These philosophers are affected either directly, indirectly, or both. During the Renaissance, Seneca's letter and Enchiridion, both of which were Stoics books, leaned towards Stoicism and were read widely, e.g., De Offissis by Cicero. Christianity sympathized with Stoicism more than Epicureanism. The Epicureans choice to support pleasure and cosmic chaos could not mix with the ideologies of Christianity. Stoic support on materialism was rejected and highly criticized while they readily accepted Logos.

Christians have mixed feelings about Stoicism. Augustine wrote favoring words on it but later rejected it. Tertullian supported Stoicism and some Enchiridion. John and Peter Abelard also promoted it while Thomas was so critical of it. Justus Lipsius revived Stoicism during Renaissance. He was a classical philologist and humanist who published editions of Tacitus and Seneca. He explained that Christians could find help from Stoicism when in trouble but also pointed the ideologies in Stoicism that are unacceptable in Christianity.

NeoStoicism had a mixed reception. Calvi was critical of the "Novi stoic" even before Justus did as it wanted the revival of apatheia. Sellars notes that one NeoStoicism text started with a cautioning remark to stop the sharp criticism. NeoStoicism was not fully embraced as its impact is mostly from Justus and maybe some little influence from Montaigne. The essential philosopher of the modern world who was influenced by Stoicism is Spinoza. Leibniz accused him of being a sect leader with Descartes. There are some similarities between the Stoic understanding of the world and Spinoza's. In both of them, they have a God that controls nature and the universe. Well, Stoics indeed understand the cosmos as dual, but in contradicting Spinoza's concept, the "passive" and "active" principles of the Stoics were intertwined and produced unitary reality.

As Long shows us that the difference was in Spinoza's understanding that God has infinite attributes was contradictory to the Stoic's finite God. He also points out that the similarities are more if we think in terms of ethics. Due to this, Spinoza's ethics are the same as Stoics'. With that knowledge, we can look at another difference in that Spinoza declined to believe in a hidden teleology to this universe. He thought that there is no God and that nature didn't have an aim. To understand better, we can take Spinoza as the staircase leading to the Stoic system.

Lastly, we will look at the connection between Kant and the Stoic, especially duty, which beyond the consequences of a person's actions. It is As Long who points out the differences again, and Kant used reasoning to make his system while the Stoics were natural and pure at heart. This difference is also found in deontological systems and eudemonistic systems like Kant's and the Stoic's. It is only recently that they want to revive Stoicism as a realistic moral philosophy.

Chapter 7: Contemporary Stoicism

In today's world, we see revivals of Stoicism and ethics. Such works by some philosophers have revived virtue ethics as an alternative for deontological approaches. According to David Chalmers and David Bourget, their philosophy states that deontology is the leading framework with 26% followed closely by consequentialism with 24% and then lagging behind we find virtue ethics with a score of 18% and other positions getting less support. It is evident that ethics is not a recognition contest, but the above percentages show that the revival of virtue ethics in today's philosophy and biographies happens at a constant rate. Specifically, Stoicism works are more pronounced, and they appear at a high standard. Some examples are Inwood 2003, Brower 2014, Graver 2007, McGlynn 2009, Goodman 2012, and many more.

We can also say that Stoicism is going back to its roots as ancient Stoics upheld their systems as practical guidance for day to day life experiences and not theoretical. Epictetus did not mince his words to try and hide his contempt for theoretical philosophies. He stated that the theories taught us how to examine arguments and to attain the skills people need to assess logic, but in reality and practicality, what we say today as users might be wrong tomorrow. We can find the roots of modern Stoicism from Frankl's logotherapy and Albert Ellis. Stoicism is not a therapy but a philosophy, and some philosophers like John Sellars, Lawrence Barker, and William Irvine gave examples of 21st century Stoicism. All of these philosophers attempted to separate the philosophical denotation of "stoic" from Stoic as a common English word that shows a person who walks in this life with a stiff upper lip. Despite the differences, there are similarities in both; for instance, they both emphasize endurance.

Becker and Irvine explained well their attempts to revive Stoicism for today's modern society. Irvine contributed that some things like actions and our judgment are up to us, while others like the past and natural occurrences we have no control of. He also noted that we have partial control over several other things. To explain more about Irvine's philosophy, we can take an example of a baseball. For the results of the baseball game, we have part control; we can play well or poorly and influence the results, but some variables we have no control of like the impartiality of the referee. In such a game, your aim should not be to win but to do your best since that is what you have control over.

Becker expounded on it better. He notes that there are differences between the ancient Stoicism and the modern one. Becker and Irvine's attempts to revive Stoicism will be determined by future philosophies and the birth of popular movements. Since the early 21st century, we have seen significant growth in that movement. We have several blogs dedicated to modern Stoicism, e.g., Stoicism Today. We also have a considerable emergence of such groups in social media, e.g., Stoicism Group on Facebook.

Chapter 8: Stoics Spiritual Exercises

Practice Misfortune

It is not easy to be in the worst situation, for instance, to be the poorest person to be the ugliest person on earth. Stoics believe that it can happen that you find yourself in such misfortunes, and therefore, it is imperative to have an experience or a taste a situation with such misfortunes. For example, when you are a rich man, take a few days and assume that you are not rich but poor. Think of the kind of clothes worn by poor people, the kind of food they eat, and where they sleep, among other difficulties they experience in their state. Practice living like a poor man going through the worst experiences he goes through; do not be tempted to go back to your riches before the days you have set for the practice are over. Remember, it is not imagination; it is about doing it and practicing it.

This practice is important once in a while as it makes one not to be a slave of being in a certain condition or owning a certain property. It gives you a chance to taste both sides of life, and therefore, make you go through life without the feeling of anxiety and fear that is caused by the uncertainty of life; remember fear and anxiety only comes when you do not know about the future, it is not about the past. Practice, therefore, should be about something that you fear that could happen to you; practice using the worst-case scenarios.

Train Perception to Avoid Good and Bad

Training perception means whatever the experienced, there is always a good side of it. Stoics believe that when a person is faced with problems, he or she can overturn the bad experience or problem into an opportunity to get experience good things. One of the stoics, Epictetus, said that every man has resources within him or her that can help in coping with any challenge. For instance, when one goes through a painful experience, he or she develops endurance; a characteristic that is required may be in the future.

Sometimes we are disappointed by the turnout of events, which drains a lot of energy from our bodies; in this case, you lose and stain yourself mentally and physically. Instead of going through all these strenuous experiences, it is better to accept the situation and everything surrounding it, and exercise virtue; at least you will become better after the experience. It is not easy to accept everything that brings disappointments, but step by step accept that everything happens for you to be better, and it is only you to take the opportunity to grow and enjoy every minute of it.

Accepting the negative experience and turning it into an opportunity is all about perception. The stoic practice involves going past your first perception about a certain happening; tie it down to enable yourself to see things being the problem. For example, your mother dies when you are still a teenager, and according to you, you still needed her around because you have not yet matured enough to take care of yourself. However, beyond the loss, there is an opportunity for you to now become a mature and responsible person. Therefore, when you experience difficulties, you can always choose the best option that will help you to become a better person.

Remember – It's All Ephemeral

Stoics do not take everything they own to be more important or use their achievements to make themselves look big. Remember the close friend or family member that you loved very much, he or she was taken away from you: he or she died. Remember the prominent people in the world, the founder of Apple company, the scientists who discovered the scientific laws that are still in use today; they all died despite their achievement and prominence. This means that even with your achievements, you are very small, and your body and mind that you used to get all that is taken from you. The rich in the world also die living their properties; you cannot be tied to your possessions forever. This means that all that you have on earth are not yours, and therefore, just consider them as borrowed things. When you borrow something from a friend, you do not hold on it so much; you use it a return it to the owner. Similarly, all things on earth should be considered as borrowed, and therefore, only use them when you have them; do not hold on them or develop an attachment because, within no time, you can lose all of them.

It is, therefore, useless to feel anger for something you were denied or something that was precious to you and destroyed by another person. Do not hurt others because you are the richest man on earth, the prominent politician, or the famous football player. It is all nothing or very small, and within no time, you can lose them, and your name will only be read in books. therefore, it is important to practice that before you hurt someone or do unthinkable because of a property you love so much, remember that all is not yours, including your body, friends, and family members.

Take the View From Above

Stoics like looking at life at a wider view, which is known as looking from above. Looking from above is being at a place that is high in the sky and seeing so many things that are in your habitat, which is the earth. You can only take that view if you are out of this world, I mean, when you are dead. In that state, on the earth, you will see the animals, water in the lakes, oceans, and rivers, soils, and plantation. There is a variety of creations, but some are in extinction. Looking at the earth, one would visualize the people who have gone through the same world, those who are still alive on those who will be there in the coming years. Some you have never seen them, and yet you live with them in the same world, and the ones who will live in the coming years, you will never see them. Looking at everything you realize that there must be a role you played on the earth, was it big or was it small that it did not have an impact on the earth and all the things and non-living things. You cannot turn back times to relive the life that you lived before you died so as you make the impact that you feel is big enough to influence life on the earth. This means that when you have lived life, there is no need to dwell on what has already passed; the only thing that you can change is the life that you are living today, and therefore, only appreciate what was done in the past and appreciate it.

This exercise helps you to look at things from a wider perspective and is always used by those who aspire to live a better life than the one they lived in the past. The mistake most people do is that when they make a small mistake, they dwell on it, forgetting that they still have a life ahead of them; regrets only pull you behind, and therefore, only focus on the most important things, which can change your life. The exercise and practice that lets you look at life without making a conclusion about your own life by looking at the past; look at it on a wider perspective by first appreciating what life offers you in the present and maximize on the opportunity you have to be happy, achieve what you can within the time you are remaining with on the earth.

You can also look at life from a wider perspective by looking at the misfortune of others. You are still alive while other people are dead, you are healthy while others are fighting for their life on the life-saving machine. You are happy with your spouse; though you are poor, we have some people who live in a palatial house, and yet they know no peace. You might be looking at your life and think that yours is a miserable life, but when you look at other people, you will realize that life has given you much more than you deserve, and therefore, just appreciate and make good out of it.

Memento Mori (Meditate on Your Mortality)

Meditating on your mortality is reminding yourself that you will not live forever, and no one knows the day they would die. Therefore, each day, you should meditate about your death like now. If I were to die right now, how will I be like in terms of my deeds? This, though, makes one think about what they say and what they do in their lives. The meditation reminds you can die anytime and, therefore, do not waste any minute of your life, use it to do a good thing, and make other people happy.

Some people criticize this exercise by saying that it makes death as the end of everything, and yet it is not. However, it is not only those who are about to die that hurry to make life purposeful and full of good things. The practice is meant to remind you of ding good things every day; thus, it helps you to live the life that you desire. This is a life that is full of goodness and fulfillment.

Spent more time with the people that God has given you, do that thing that you are postponing at the moment because you are not sure of tomorrow. This exercise helps also to manage time well and make use of the chances provided to us all the time.

Is This within My Control

Our happiness is determined by the things that we can control and those that we cannot control. It is imperative to know the things that are within your control and those that are not. In life, the things that we cannot control are too many of those that we can control. For instance, we cannot fully control what can happen to us, the people that surround us, and what they do and say. We cannot fully control the health of our bodies and our preferences, among many other things. The thing that is controlled by us is the way we think and perceive the things that we see, hear, and taste. Therefore, the secret is that you can control our happiness by changing the perception of things.

If you can distinguish or identify the things that you can control and the ones that you cannot, then it will be easier to live a stress-free life. When faced with a situation, it is, therefore, good to exercise through having a conversation with yourself, asking yourself if whatever you are dealing with is in your control or not. For instance, you are moving to a new neighborhood and because it will have neighbors who got there before you and those who will find you there. Therefore, you have no control over the king of neighbor that you should have, and this should not worry you. Just develop a positive attitude towards the neighbors that you have and the ones you might have in the future and try to cope with them. Again, you are not fully sure putting on the right attitude will surely lead to a good neighborhood because you have an idea if they will notice your effort and reciprocate. Therefore, just be happy that you have the right attitude, and the rest will just fall in place.

Journal

The day is always full of many activities, and some of the activities are repetitive in nature. You realize that if the activities are repetitive, if you do not look at the critically the way you do them, there is a likelihood that you will do the same thing over and over, probably repeating the mistakes or doing it incorrectly every day. Some people wonder why they do not grow socially, intellectually, and economically. This is because they do not have a routine of keeping daily journals of what they have done during the day.

Journaling should not only include what you have done during the day but also how you have done it. The journal should also show a list of good things that you have done, and those that you think that you have not done well could be given a description of how better you can improve to make it better. Improving yourself is striving to be a better person every day, and therefore, your daily journal on how you have improved and where you plan to improve and how you plan to do it should also be recorded.

All the record in the journal helps you in growth. The part on the good thing that you have done gives you motivation; when you do something good, it brings positive energy on your side, giving you a forward force that will enable you to do more good tomorrow and in the future. The part for what you have not done well gives an indication that you should improve; it gives information on the specific aspects that you are supposed to improve on. The reflection on what you have not done well gives brings about critical thinking that gives options on how to improve and helps to evaluate the options to find out the better option.

Having this exercise at the end of every day is important as it motivates an individual to strive to be a better person. It also shows progress as the daily evaluation helps to know what you have achieved and what you have not. It also acts as a guide to what one wants to achieve in the future.

Practice Negative Visualization

Everyone is expected to be positive about the future and not think about negative outcomes. It is called keeping positive energy. This is not the case when it comes to stoicism. Stoicism allows an individual to practice negative visualization because it is not everything that would be positive even if you have done everything right. This exercise helps an individual to imagine the things that might go wrong in the future and prepare for them in case they happen. This exercise starts by looking at the plans that you have in the future and reviewing them one by one, and rehearsing how they would be done and the required resources. The people involved in the plans should also be looked at and their availability; remember, if you are going for a long journey using a car, the driver of your car might get sick along the way, even if he has taken all the precautions and his or her body is in good condition. Also, people have their plans, and when you plan to include them in yours, their availability must be conformed and planned for, but it does not mean that they will be there for you. This does not mean that your plans stop, always have an alternative. Therefore, you should take care of the eventualities by having another driver with you.

This exercise ensures that you put everything into its place; somebody said that failing to plan is planning to fail. You should not allow failure to find you; plan for it so that if it arises, you have ways to go around it. Failure also makes people frustrated, and depending on the personality and how serious it has affected you, it can have an effect on your mental health; having control of the future and the negative happening expected makes you have control of the future.

Amor Fati (Love Everything That Happens)

Sometimes we regret or feel bad when something happens, and it is not in our favor. It is not easy to control what happens in the world; therefore, it is better to embrace the attitude that what happens is for a reason and when it happens, do not worry about how it happens; be happy, regardless of whether it has happened in your favor or not. People who practice stoicism concentrate only on what they can control, and the events of anything that they cannot control; they leave it to fate. When something that is out of control happens, it is a reality because it is already done, and therefore accepting it is the only thing one can do. Accepting it means that it should not bring unhappiness to anyone, and instead, one is supposed to love it the way it is. The essence of this attitude is that, even if you become unhappy about it, there is nothing you can do about it; you cannot turn back times to undo the action, and even if you do, still you cannot do it differently because you have no control over the situation.

Some things, which are to happen in the future, also exhibit the same characteristics. Even if you struggle with all your energy, fate will remain the same. Therefore, there is no need to strain yourself for it. For example, when you are going for an interview, and you are stuck in traffic, there is nothing you can do if that is the only route and means of transport to the interview location. Even if you walk, it will take you more hours, and you will still be late. The only thing is to accept the fact that you are going to be late and pray that whatever happens when you reach the location of the interview will be in your favor. However, if it does not work out to your favor, just accept it as good and feel happy again, because you have no control over the situation. Holding on the event makes you miserable; things happen, and they pass; therefore, it is not healthy to attach yourself to what you wanted to happen or what you like.

Chapter 9: Stoicism Is Ideal for the Real World

In the past chapters, we have already had an in-depth glimpse of stoicism and how it came to be. We have looked at the history and background of stoicism, not forgetting the Greek and Roman stoicism. This chapter focuses on the relationship that stoicism has with the real world. As we have earlier seen, stoicism refers to the non-display of feelings even when you are going through so much.

The stoics in a bid to develop practical guidance for everyday life developed three disciplines by the use of ethics, physics, and logic. Logic forms a basis when it comes to sane thinking and making a sound judgment. This basis is requisite in order to decode the next arms. We move on to physics. Physics entails the comprehension of human nature, and how the world is composed is a basic element in a bid to secure how the world works. When we have a basis for this, we are able to lead our lives in the best way possible. Which is known as ethics? The guidance was then divided into three disciplines, namely, assent, desire, and action. This was the works on one Epictetus. Although there exist these distinctions, all three of them marry each other.

Epictetus explains three things that a man ought to associate themselves with if they want to be mentally apt. What we desire and what we averse. This is in a bid to ensure that you get what you desire, and you do not get into what you averse. This involves careful living. Second, comes locomotion. This is how an individual moves about. It involves not falling into recklessness. Thus staying careful in whatever you do. The third is that of assent. Assent entails not displaying your emotions even at the worst of events.

Assent as a Discipline

The discipline known as assent corresponds with logic. The discipline has an effect of creating a distinction between the behavior of human beings of reason and animals. This is because it entails the process of sheer seeking knowledge, which often leads to acquiring it, then decoding the knowledge. According to the Stoics, human beings get knowledge from what they may have experienced in the past. Moreover, they buy from the school of thought that as social beings of nature, we have some inborn predetermined concepts that gauge our moral behavior. Before we grant or deny something, we use reason in order to make a judgment. This judgment is often a result of assenting to something or failing to do so. This has also been referred to as phrenosis. Phrenosis refers to the process by which an individual is able to employ practical wisdom in his everyday activities. This entails making the right decision whenever necessary. Today the act of using practical though can be referred to as mindfulness. Mindfulness entails making the right decision whenever necessary.

We are encountered with various events in our lives, and what is of concern is not the event rather but how we respond towards the event. Take, for instance; somebody does something wrong with you. You will be inclined to respond in any manner that you wish. Although you have to keep in mind that every response has a consequence. Your mind as a tool is what decides what goes on throughout your day. Your mind will be the reason you engage in various activities and why you respond to various stimuli the way you do. The consequences of your actions will always follow you down the road. This discipline relates to the right thoughts and the implication of reason in order to guide oneself.

The discipline of assent manifests itself in various ways in our lives. Take, for instance, you are driving down the alley, and a pick-up truck comes and hits your bumper and then drives off quickly. Your first reaction towards the incident will be to come to an emergency stop. You will then curse the driver who was in the pick-up truck as he or she drives away. When you heard the hit at the back of your vehicle, you came to an abrupt stop. This is what is referred to as the use of emotions in a correct manner. You were shaken because things were not in their status quo, and thus, you decided to stop and make sure. When you rested assured you were safe, the feeling of anger came out as depicted by the loathsome quarrels that you let out towards the pick-up truck driver. The anger comes in as a result of using emotions in the wrong way. The events have already taken place, and there is no need for you to be angry at this point.

Anger will only serve as a disadvantage to you because you will be emotional and thus easy to make mistakes. The rage can make you affect more accidents. The stoics related thinking according to nature with living according to nature. This involves the correct use of your mind in making rational decisions. The process of thinking was thus divided into two. This involved one that was according to emotions, thus intuitive thinking and another that is according to reason.

Desire as a Discipline

The discipline of desire can be linked to control. We all have an understanding of what desire is. Desire refers to the want of something. When you desire something, you are in complete want of that thing.

The idea that lies beneath the discipline of desire is easily comprehended. In life, we are defined by our social classes and our abilities in one way or another. No matter how hard we try to overshadow this fact, this is the veracity of what happens. For instance, there are things that are in our control and those that are not. Those that are in our control, we are able to manipulate them in a manner that we desire, but those that are not, we can do very little about them. For instance, there are things that are under our direct manipulation. This includes but is not limited to: reactions, desires, and judgment. There are things that are not in our control, however. We try to control these things by giving it our all. This may include our goals, the ones that we set in order to achieve. They may be long term or short term. There is often a fifty-fifty chance of succeeding, thus when engaging in something; it is of great essence to consider the odds. The odds may not always be in your favor, sometimes the situation may change, and you need to know how to respond when this happens.

Many religious topics have related to this topic by drawing reference from their various prayers. For instance, a prayer seeking God to give us the calm in accepting who we are and what we cannot change. We fall into a deep depression, usually because we want to influence changes in what we have no power over. We care much about what others think about us and not what we want for ourselves. Our friend's feelings and opinions are out of our scope of what we can influence. We have no control over that. Focusing on that will often bring you stress because you will not get the desired results.

Imagine a scenario where you are about to go for an interview. Here you need to focus on the things that are going to be a plus one to your resume. If you let your anxiety disorient you to an extent whereby you are in the worry of the interviewee, how they may react to your responses, you shift your desires to a place where you have no control over whatsoever. The feelings of the interviewees are born with them, and they will stay with them. Your manipulation is not in their jurisdiction. Your best approach can be to focus on how best you will do your part. This will play a big role in aiding you to move closer to your job. Creative thinking is a method by which you engage your mind in the sheer analysis of thoughts that will build upon your situation.

Desire needs to be tamed in order to fit in the shoes of our capability. Taming of desire requires meditation peacefully. You are in your own world, and you can visualize what you are in the reach of and what you are not. Meditation also brings you to the present and relates you to the situations at hand. You are aware of what is not in your control, and thus you can respond positively towards it. Our ability to stay present to the current situations is heightened. When we embrace the act of being present, decision making becomes easier for us.

Action as a Discipline

We all engage in various actions as a result of various triggers that manifest themselves in our lives. Right action is often rare.

People will act on impulse and regret after. Your response thus, your action has to be cultivated in a manner that suggests you have a sense of direction. An action combined with another action will often lead to greater action. In order to achieve something great, you need to do things step by step. Often you have heard someone refer to the saying of a journey of a thousand miles. Persistence and perseverance are what wins the day. When you achieve one action at a time, you will realize the magnitude of this at the end of the day.

Boldness and courage are what is embraced when performing an action. Shyness would often cause the action not to effect. The force applied in action is not a raw force. It is a skilled force directed towards your best interest. Why do we act? We do this in response to various triggers to our pressure points, forcing us to give up our stationary nature and adopt one that is locomotive. This is the definition of right action. When we are faced with obstacles in our lives, the solution often lies with the right action.

There include three facets that act as an aid when determining the right action to take. They include meeting rhythms, metrics, and priorities. With these tools, you are in a position to have a forecast about what will happen in the future. You can weigh the consequences of an action before engaging in them.

Priority helps you to weigh your problems in a hierarchy. This hierarchy enables you to weigh your problems in a manner from the one that requires an immediate response to the others that can wait. This way, you are able to solve your problems systematically. You do not dwell so much on the problems that have a lower implication in your life. Metrics will entail the analysis of the consequences. With this, you are able to anticipate the consequences. Metrics, in its sense, entails measuring the diversity of something. With metrics at hand, you are able to act accordingly and in the right manner. You will always way your options before settling for a particular option. Your actions will not be rush but rather well-thought through. Metrics will also be of advantage in your everyday life. When you weigh your options correctly, you are in a position whereby you will not find yourself in trouble all the time.

With meeting rhythms, the same way you are ready in the face of trouble, you will be waiting for opportunities to knock on your door in order to maximize on them. You will not overlook opportunities, and you tread carefully and smart. Trading smart has an effect on making an individual succeed in whatever he or she is doing. When you are faced with trouble, you will be in analysis of the various responses you can assume and be ready to take any when the need arises. Taking action is often thought through process and not by an event.

Chapter 10: Manage Your Emotions to Find Inner Peace

We encounter various instances in our lives, and how we respond normally is a reflection of how we feel. How we best to control our emotions will have an effect on how we respond positively to various situations. There are various techniques that we can use in order to manage our emotions.

Practice Deep Breathing

Science has it that when you take a deep breath, you increase the production of endorphins that will result in heightened brain activity. This way, you are able to feel less tensed and anxious. Fresh breath carries with it a fresh supply of oxygen, which is important in keeping your brain apt. Simple breathing programs have been seen to be great relievers of stress. You can make a habit of doing these exercises whenever you feel like your emotions will overwhelm you. Before engaging in a breathing exercise, there are a number of things that you need to consider. The spot for this exercise should be a comfortable place. Your mode of clothing should be one that does not cause distraction. Deep breathing will come on its own, and it is a need-not force issue. You do not force deep breathing, but rather, it comes on its own. This practice can be done twice a day. These exercises do not last for long in that they will not take much of your time.

A misconception that has always prevailed with people is that they tend to take shallow breaths as a remedy for deep breaths. Shallow breaths have the effect of shutting you down. Your energy is shut down with short, shallow breaths because they tend to increase the anxiety rather than diminish it. Imagine you are panting like a dog in the face of trouble, this may even end up with you passing out. Before you get on with the breathing process, take note that you should: Make sure you are comfortable, it can be a horizontal posture with a pillow under your neck, or it could be a seated posture on a chair with your head and shoulders supported.

When breathing, let air flow in through your nostrils, let it fill your lung cavity, your ribcage will always respond by enlarging while your air sacs will be filled with air. When breathing out, it should be through your nose too. In order to feel this movement effectively, you need to put one hand on your stomach and the other on the chest. You need to do this repeatedly in order to achieve the desired results. The process of breathing should be one that encompasses the brain too. While breathing, make sure that you are keen enough to focus. You engaged in the breathing exercise in order to feel relieved. In order to achieve this relief, you need to close your eyes and picture an image that brings out the best feelings in you. This will be often reflective, or it can take another form.

Surround yourself with peace. In order to achieve this, you need to imagine that the air around you is warm and welcoming. When you do this, you will visualize this peace from its entry point to your body until the time that it exits the body. You feel the airflow all the way. In this manner, you are also able to visualize your troubles as they leave you, and you separate yourself from it. You can consider embracing the use of a phrase in order to maximize the effects. The procedure can take an average of ten to twenty minutes in maximum. The lengths of the breaths should be increased as you advance in your routine. This achieves more results.

When breathing, makes sure that your muscles also participate. Practice a routine whereby as you take in air, you contract your muscles in a bid to feel tensed. Release this grip as you exhale. Your muscles should relax in synchrony, flowing the systematic arrangement from the feet all the way to the head. Each muscle should be tensed at a time in order to achieve maximum results. This way, the muscles participate, too, and you are able to achieve maximum relaxation. Your last breath should be the one that pushes all your troubles away.

Find Your Inner Power

When we are in the face of trouble, linking ourselves to our inner strength will see to it that we rise from the trouble, and we are able to move forward. There are a number of ways that will see to it that you connect to your inner self and that you are able to rise. The various success stories that have come from numerous people who were able to connect themselves with their inner power. For instance, below are some exercises that will see to it that your inner strength is elicited and that you are able to use it in a manner that is advantageous to you.

Believe in yourself

When we do not believe in ourselves, we are insecure about the occurrence of a particular set of facts. This is because we have not accepted in ourselves that we can be accepted because of our various strengths. Various strengths will manifest themselves with side effects as weaknesses. When we are insecure, our inner strength is diminished greatly. In order to achieve believing in yourself, you need to practice accepting who you are. When you have feelings of like towards yourself, you are able to like the world around you more.

Practice Silence

We live in a world that you may not know what is going on in somebody's life. Due to these distinctions, the world is filled with confusion every now and then. This can be a distraction to you when you are focusing on achieving your own self goals. Taking some time to stay in silence plays a big role in making you refreshed. Furthermore, you are isolated from people, and you can think on your feet. Silence means that you are devoid of anything that elicits noise. This means no technology should be involved. When you achieve silence, your inner chaos is calmed, and you are able to connect with the strength that exists inside you.

Repetitive Program

We often do things in a shoddy manner because our inner energy has been drained. When an ounce of our physical energy is used up, our inner strength is also used up. The effect is direct. You want to find your inner self, and the best way you can do this is through separating the activities you engage in daily into separate simple and achievable portions that you can achieve progressively throughout the day. When you do this, you are in a position to do these tasks in a repetitive manner, and with this, you can achieve mastery. When you achieve mastery, your brain is at ease. When your brain is at ease, you have created a lot of space in it.

Check on your circle

We respond in discrepancy, especially when we are around various people. The same way that different people have a way of making us feel in some type of way. When you are around a bad company, your inner energy will always be diminished when you meet them. They fill you with information that has a tolling effect on your inner energy. They often dwell on filling you with their inadequacies, which in turn will make you feel sucked off the juice in life. Look for people who have a positive impact on your life. People who will make you bring out the best in you. Optimism is what you look for when you are seeking a circle. There are people who feed you with positive energy. This type of energy is important in building the inner you. Most of the time, after a conversation with these guys, you will find that you have cultivated a culture of thinking positively, which boosts your inner strength.

Impression

Research has it that what you feel inside will often find its way to the surface. The vice versa also works as what is perceived in the outside is a representation of what is on the inside. Exercising and feeding properly will see to it that you remain proper in the outside. Your dressing should be also in a manner that makes you feel best about yourself. When you are concerned about your health, you are in a position to make sure that your body is in good condition. Ti refers to both internally and externally. The body comprises numerous parts, some of which need keen consideration in order to know when they are in jeopardy. When you create a good example on the outside, you are in a position to influence your inner self the same way. This way, you boost your confidence.

Link with Your Energy Source

The spiritual sphere has been seen to be the most effective when I come to connect to your inner self. This is not limited to one religious sphere, but rather it is diverse. Meditation will link you to your inner energy when done in repetition. Meditation is key because, during this time, you visualize yourself as being alone. In order to effectively exhibit your inner strength, you need to create a link with the spheres that surround you. The sphere around you is greater than you, and this is what puts it in a position whereby it can multiply your inner strength. When your inner strength is multiplied, it has an effect on your physical strength too. You believe that you are in a position whereby you can achieve more even though your physical energy does not say the same story.

Focusing on Self-Love

On the basis of love is the feeling of self -love. This is because you cannot claim to extend the feelings of love to another person until you extend them to yourself. Self-love is at the peak of healthy living. This is because it will be a determinant of the many factors that will stick with you all the way. Self-love does not merely entail the feeling of good. This is more than that. This is being in a position to appreciate yourself from a deeper context. Self-love manifests itself in the doings that make our lives worth living. When we appreciate our lives, we are in a position to appreciate ourselves, and it is only then that we will start to appreciate others. Actions that make us grow are what make self-love possible. The diversity of self-love extends to how well we accept our inadequacies. How we adapt and live with them all our lives appreciating the fact that we are human. The acceptance of human nature is one that entails a keen understanding that we have shortcomings just as we have strengths. In order to achieve self-love, there are some pointers that an individual may use. They include:

Mindfulness

Mindfulness is directly attached to self-love because people who practice mindfulness are in a position to take note of how they feel, what they want, and what they are thinking. They are careful enough not to trade on the grounds that will have an effect on them. Mindful people will think through an event before deciding to take part. They will analyze a situation in terms of consequences even before they decide to engage.

Priority

Priority is key when practicing self-love. With priority, you are assured of satisfying your urgent needs before you proceed o wants and not vice versa. This concept may seem remote, yet it carries a higher concept. There are people who participate in impulse buying; these types of people will always acquire what they see when they like it without an inner contemplation. With priority, you will be able to analyze the situations at hand in terms of wants and needs and as a result, find the perfect criteria in which you can acquire goods.

Self-Care

Self-care is at the bedrock of self-love. When you care about yourself, the effect is often that you will extend some degree of care towards yourself. Often people who have been found not to extend some degree of care towards themselves have been said to have no love towards themselves. This is because care and love go hand in hand.

Boundaries

Creating boundaries goes a long way in trying to exhibit self-love. When you create boundaries, you are in a position not to be affected by the emotions of other people. When we get carried away in the emotions of others, you will get angry at yourself all the time. You will be concerned about the feelings of others rather than yourself. This way, you do not love yourself.

Gratitude to oneself

Gratitude entails being thankful for all that facilitates your well-being. Gratitude can be directed to oneself or to other people.

Gratitude has some aspects of mindfulness in that it will entail the recognition of the deed before gratitude can ensue. A reflection on the topic of gratitude will often make people think of materialistic gratitude. People view gratitude as a great thing and often forget that it can go as basic. When you are kind to other people, that is a simple way of expressing your gratitude. No matter how remote this act may seem, it often has implications that are deep-rooted. What sits in between a totally awesome day and a bad day is the distinguishing acts of gratitude.

Self-gratitude happens in a bid to appreciate oneself; it could be through the situations that you have had in life. Self-gratitude happens as a result of a monologue with oneself, telling yourself that you have so much to be thankful about. Self-gratitude is also buried deep under the concepts of self-care and self-love. Practicing gratitude is as easy as it may be and is also as effective as possible when done in the right manner. A single word of gratitude said to someone will often go a long way. You give gratitude to yourself because you are in a better position of noticing your life advance than others. Most of the time, you may expect to receive gratitude from others, and when this is not the case, we tear down in emotional disgust. Being grateful to oneself boosts the overall confidence of an individual. When the confidence of an individual is boosted, the individual is in a better position to achieve more in life.

Self-gratitude can be a daily routine, something that you do to remind yourself how great you are. In order to achieve self-gratitude, you need to have a gratitude statement, one that you repeat daily. In order to achieve more, you need to set achievable goals, which are short term and work on achieving them step by step. Make sure that you take note of inspirational quotes that are effective in building your self-esteem at the onset of the day and throughout the day. Approach a reflective outlook whereby you focus on how far you have come. Looking back at your past experiences play an important role in helping you to move forward from your previous experiences.

Forgive Easily

To some people, according to forgiveness to someone is easy, whereas to others, it takes more than the words. Egotistic people will often feel like they do not wish to exhibit forgiveness, whether it is asking for it or offering it. In order to adopt a culture of forgiveness, there are a number of things that you need to take note of: When you are wronged, you will first experience anger, which will seek to take control of your body. Anger makes us decide on a no basis manner. This is often because we feel that we have the ever-rising need to respond. When we are wrong, we ought to take some time and let the anger flow past you before you can be able to respond. Normally the response to anger is spontaneous and may often result in a consequence that you did not desire.

In order to effectively forgive someone, you need not rush the process as forgiveness is a gradual adventure that ought to take steps before you can effectively say that you have forgiven someone. When granting forgiveness, one ought not to feel obligated, but rather, this needs to be a good feeling one that elicits good vibes. Before forgiveness, one needs to practice acceptance that the set of facts are the way they are and will not change. We need to change to adopt overriding circumstances. Acceptance is processed by which you are directing your thoughts towards finding a remedy to what has already taken place. Forgiving can be life-changing if you set your mind to it, and you do it.

People often draw feelings from their past. From these feelings, they carry experiences that made them feel that way in the past. An individual will feel bad when the same kind of story keeps on repeating itself in his or her life. Imagine the same grievance happening to you all over. This I possibly an indication that you did not forgive and move on. Forgiveness entails distancing yourself from the narrowest of thoughts that arouse past experiences that may make you not forgive. Though forgiveness may take some deep reframing, it is worth it in order to effect recovery.

With forgiveness, you focus on the events taking place at the moment, and you stay devoid of the past. Feelings of the occurrence might be depressing. This is what makes you even reconsider forgiveness. Allow the stress to leave you. When you achieve this, you are in a position to let go through forgiving. Breathing deeply can help a great deal when wanting to control the effects of something. This will calm your body and mind leaving you devoid of stress. When you are devoid of stress, you are able to make a sound judgment. Forgiveness is a gradual process. The moment we understand this is when we will easily achieve it.

Chapter 11: Ways to Manage Anger Using Stoicism

Because of the emphasis of Stoicism on understanding your emotions, anger comes on top as an emotion that we could use to manage how we feel.

In the book *The Meditations*, philosopher Marcus Aurelius detailed on how we could use Stoicism to help us manage our anger better. In the book, he outlined ten different strategies with which we could manage our anger. They were gifts, he said from the Greek God of healing, Apollo, and his nine muses.

Remember That You Are Not Perfect Either

Stoics considered it paramount that to adhere to the therapy of the philosophy, one needed to come to terms with their flaws.

Seneca noted that anger affected even the gentlest of people and that, therefore, to effectively work on managing your passion, you needed to admit it to yourself. In the world today, cases of people going to extreme because of the rages of anger have been well documented, with examples of domestic violence, crimes of passion, and homicide lending credence to this fact. Therefore, you would want to lay your anger on someone means that you, therefore, are not in tune with who you are.

The view by Seneca, therefore, means that to use Stoicism would require that you take a pause and think of how you would potentially do things to people that would get them angry. It called that while you pointed your finger at another person, the other three were led back at you, and therefore, you were at risk to be at fault just as much as the other person was.

So this call for us to admit that we were just as likely to commit the offense done to us would then make us take a step back and view the situation more calmly and rationally.

Aristotle believed that anger was not all bad and was justified in some instances. Therefore, when you acknowledged this, you would be able to realize then that another person's anger, therefore, would be justified. Therefore, by admitting to yourself that you are not a perfect being would mean that you would also become more willing to extend empathy to the other person, as you will know that, had you been in their shoes, as offended as they are, you most likely would have reacted the same, or similarly.

Thus, when you become more in-tune with your faults as a human being, then chances are high that you will prioritize the need to view the other person through non-judgmental lenses. When someone steps on your shoes, you then admit to yourself that it is a mistake that you also would have made.

However, this admitting of wrong does not mean that becomes willing to let people get away with being incorrigible assholes. Indeed, it would make you better at assessing people and bringing you more in touch with the essence of humanity and, thus, become more able to see others through better lenses.

It's Not the Behavior That Upsets You, and It's Your Opinion About It

One of the most important questions that you can ask yourself is that -is it that specific behavior makes you angry, or is it the person?

One of the ways we show cognitive dissonance when it comes to emotional responses, and most importantly anger, is that depending on the context, we tend to allow or let go of a particular behavior even when we admit to ourselves that we do not tolerate the behavior.

Look at it this way. You visit the park; a place is teeming with people. You join the others in making the best of your time there. Then, a confrontation between one of the employees of the parks and a visitor ensues. It's a shouting match and threatens to come to blow. You look at the two as people unable to control their anger. You learn of what led to the blow-up and are not impressed. So, you point at a castigating finger at them. But, supposing it was a friend, would you castigate them too? Chances are, you would possibly defend them, feeling their anger was justified because you understand the context.

When put in context, the reason why we get angry could be down to how much emphasis we place on particular behavior and traits. For this reason, then, you will find that some things will make you angry but not make another person upset, or it could make another person angry but not you.

Therefore, to become better at managing your anger, knowing what makes you angry, and why is important. This would allow you to understand the context and how it influences your reaction. You will also be able to understand better why another person got angry about something that did not raise more than a curious glance from you.

Understanding how our opinions shape our emotional reaction to things is vital in developing ways in which we can become more rational and better at managing our anger. This would also allow us to come to terms with the cognitive dissonance that makes us castigate certain people when they are angry for justifiable reasons and defending others.

For stoics, this view on what drives your anger on certain things would mean that you will be able to reconcile yourself with whether you are placing too much emphasis on things that re beyond your control. Placing too much emphasis on things that you cannot control will most often result in heartbreak for you. Always. And this could make you angry even more. This could take a toll on your emotional state. As Seneca stated, we need to confront our anger as an enemy - away from the center of our emotional chambers. Allowing yourself to get angry at situations that are indifferent to your well-being would mean that you would then not make any productive progress with your anger.

Your Anger Does More Harm to you Than What You Are Angry About

How does it feel when you are angry? It's so - draining, right? There you are, apoplectic and exploding like volcanoes. Your heart is racing violently, sending tearing sensations through your chest like it's about to burro itself out of your sternum. Your body trembles and you are barely breathing fine. Your head thuds and your thoughts grind to a halt. All you see, then, is what made you angry. This is certainly not the best feeling.

Now, of course, there are medical repercussions to getting angry, which include, but not limited to, HBP.

According to Stoics, anger makes you ugly. It distorts your features and makes you an unpleasant grotesques creature that is cringy to look at, and we don't want that. But of course, being unpleasant to look at is not the end of it. This is just as a start, and perhaps you are already ugly, so this effect doesn't affect you much. Well, there is a reason this point doesn't end here.

Consider this scenario. You buy a new phone which you have been saving for months. You are ecstatic and jubilant. Wow! Its features are just astounding. You float away to your friends. You want to show off your new phone. And you get there, and they are all happy for you. It goes on well until one of your friends, as they attempt to take a selfie, drops it to the ground. The screen shatters, and with it shatters too your dream of spending some quality time with your new phone. You are livid! You accuse your friend of jealousy and stomp out.

Your anger clouds your mind, and you do not take note that you are ruining the friendship. According to Stoics, other people's actions that make us angry only harm our outside – our possessions, maybe our bodies – but when we are angry, we harm our very core. Anger clouds our better judgment, which would make us react in a manner than injures our character. By limiting our ability to reason, anger could be the reason why you lose friendships and relationships. It could be what costs you your jobs.

When you understand that what you are angry about is something that you could deal with and still maintain your character, you become able to then deal with it productively.

Before letting anger take control of you, begin by thinking about what it will cost you and whether that is more important than what is making you angry at that moment. Chances are, what is making you angry is not worth your character. It is not worth indulging in the draws of anger if it will result in you losing people you love and value. It is not worth indulging if it will cost you your job.

Marcus Aurelius went as far as to state that one needed not to be angry at people that they consider kin, as this went against the Stoic Principle of Nature that said that we should work together. This means then that you should never let your anger overtake your love for the people close to you. Speaking broadly, we can also interpret this view as not to be angry with our fellow human beings.

They May Not Understand Why It's Wrong

Socrates once stated that no human being did evil in their knowledge. As such, when someone wrongs us, the natural impulse is for us to seek then ways in which we can take revenge on them.

In the broader view of this, people will often defend what they are doing when they are questioned about it. Concerning the countless events that have happened in the world in the past, when we look at them, the perpetrators of these heinous acts felt that they were doing the right thing. They weren't harming other human beings, you see, they were defending their people. In their twisted way, they felt that they were doing the right thing. This view is controversial and seems to justify why the people committed it. But this view is to instead bring to the surface how we will defend what we do in our heads.

Seneca summarized this view when he gave an example of how one would not kick a donkey back or how one would not bite back a dog because the man felt that they did not know what they were doing. As such, he called for us to extend this to our fellow human beings then. Rather than respond to anger with anger, he called for us to rid ourselves of it and then make a point of trying to rid of the other person of it too.

Our need to condemn and vilify people that offend us could be counterproductive in that we may find ourselves exhibiting the same blind spot when in a different situation where we are the angry one.

Once more, understanding that someone doing wrong could not be aware of how wrong it is not to justify the fact that they are wrong. Instead, it is to bring ourselves much closer to how we act and react when confronted by a situation or right and wrong that we may not be aware of.

As such, rather than repay wrong with our anger, this calls for us to make an effort to make the person more knowledgeable on why their actions were illegal and why they will need to change. This view is what is shaping the current movement in many countries to make prisons reformative rather than punitive. To punish one who did not know why their actions were wrong would only make them more likely to do the wrong deed again. They would have anger, which would make what they do feel justifiable, thus, creating a vicious cycle of anger birthing anger.

Even in Anger, Be Compassionate

The above point segues directly into this one.

When someone wrongs you, it only becomes natural that you will then see it fit that you punish them. In trying to punish them later, you put yourself in a situation where you become angry too, and again, in punishing them, you make them mad and spiraling from this, generations of anger.

Aurelius stated that when someone made him angry, what he would do is first dealing with the feelings of anger within. As we have learned in this chapter, this would involve understanding your imperfections and how your opinion shapes your rage. Once he had done this, Aurelius would then take the person aside and explain to then calmly, about how in their moment of anger, they were doing themselves harm and not him. This belief that an angry person deserves help or to be educated helped him then become more cool-headed into his later years.

Seneca called on us to not judge other people based on failings that all of us are bound to fall short of from time to time. He called for tolerance, making the point that, if many people had pardoned their enemies, was it not right then, to forgive someone that makes you angry by little actions?

Through calling for us to become more tolerant and patient with other people's behavior, Seneca and Aurelius then made it known that they wanted us to think through our anger before acting. Thus, it was easier to give the other person the benefit of the doubt when you took the time to process your passion before reacting to it.

A belief that, unfortunately, several people hold seems to be that showing compassion is a sign of weakness. More affected by this are many men, whose trait has been termed as toxic masculinity, which encompasses a lack of empathy, a glorification on unproductive anger among other negative characters as inherently male.

Seneca called on us to put our trust in someone that showed an understanding towards a fool. He called on us to reject the first incentive of rage, which often calls us to seek to punish the other person. Through the building of compassion, which is an inherent human emotion, we will be able to become better at managing our anger. When we make it a point to take our time to understand why someone made us angry, we then become better at putting our thought before our actions when we are mad. This helps us then become better at conflict management through de-escalation.

In Book Two of *The Meditations*, Marcus Aurelius, stated that in life, you would come across people who bore unpleasant traits, ungrateful and violent, unsociable. But such people, he said, seemed not to have the knowledge of what was good and what was bad. Instead, as a person who has taken the time to understand the implications of your actions, and especially under the intense passions of anger, you would then take the responsibility of persuading the other person on why their actions of anger were injuring them more than the people that they intended to hurt.

When you become more compassionate, you then begin to see how, indeed, in life, very few things need to get you angry. This would make you live a more fulfilling life and become better at how you treat people and how you manage tense situations.

Chapter 12: Understanding How and Why Anger Rises

That we will get angry is not something that we can debate about nor disagree with. As with other emotions within us, it will come from time to time, with varied triggers and of course, calling on us to react to it in a variety of ways. In a bid to manage our anger better, we need to understand how and why.

Understanding the Reasons Why

We get angry for very many reasons. A friend that can't stop meddling in our affairs can send us up the wall. A person that you don't like can get a rise out of you just by existing. Someone unable to take in simple instructions can raise your hackles. Therefore, learning of our triggers was key to helping us control our anger.

The reasons are as vast and different as the number of people that exist on the planet. Whether anger was justified or not is something that still has philosophers in this modern-day cross swords. Aristotle believed that anger was justified in some instances. Aristotle said that getting angry at the right time and with the right reason made anger right. But while this was true, it became hard to determine how to measure what was the right time and what counted for the right reason. As we have said above, and in chapter 11, the fact that our beliefs and our opinions about things made us then determine what made us angry makes it difficult to find common ground then.

Seneca was categorical in his belief that anger was just a vice with no redeeming quality. He viewed that passion made us slaves and that once one allowed themselves to be overtaken by the emotion, then they would not slow down.

Looking at this, it then becomes critical to us that, in a bid to make ourselves more rational and in control of our anger, understanding what makes us angry and why is essential.

This knowledge would then allow us to break through the situation where we get angered by inconsequential events or opinions. It becomes paramount then that we know the reasons for us being angry are productive and, thus, that we should then allow ourselves to feel this anger.

Getting angry at your friend for breaking your phone would be counterproductive since it would mean that you would lose a friend if you expressed your anger, on top of the fact that the consequence was external and, thus, easy to confront and conquer. However, getting angry at an injustice lends credibility to Aristotle's belief that there was a period when, indeed, we are justified to get worked up.

However, even with the understanding of good and evil, we needed to be aware of the fact that the other person could be doing the wrong from the point of ignorance, thus, approaching them with a desire to educate them rather than punish.

With is in mind, it becomes easier to know if you need to get angry or not. For the most part, anger is damaging to you, and it is best to avoid getting tangled in its tentacles.

Distancing From the Appearance

When you have seen how destructive anger is, you will begin to decide then to work on it.

Stoics then call on us to take our focus away from the physical and into the spiritual.

Seneca stated that our goal should be to attain a tranquil mind. This state, he said, made it possible for the Stoic to then remain calm in the face of a tempest of rage and fury.

Appearances can be deceiving, and thus, will mislead us into thinking that a situation requires our attention when it doesn't. Take note of when something is offered to you with seeming the express intention to make you angry. Anger, according to Seneca, is a binary emotion, taking charge of you as soon as you are well aware of it.

This then means that you would be easily swayed under its sweeping wings when you were obsessed with what was in front of you. We have seen this many times. An example of this being a scenario called 'outrage porn,' where someone, or at times the media, shares a story whose main intention is to create a rise out of people. Through cheap sentimentality and melodrama, they use this focus that we have on the efficient processing of data, meaning that we will get angry at what is directly in front of us. When you make the attainment of mental tranquility your focus then, appearances begin to matter less. When a story is shared with the express intent of making people angry, instead, you go further into the story to find out if there is any justifiable reason to get angry.

By emphasizing what is merely in front of you, you become less reactive and more in control of how you interpret things. You understand that there is more to what you are seeing. When someone is angry at you, you do not get mad at them in return, because you know that there could be more to their anger than just you. You'd also know that the violence is doing them more harm than good. You will take personal lessons from the teaching of Socrates that tell us not to do wrong or repay evil with evil, no matter how right it feels or how justifies we think we are.

Emphasizing appearances then will mean that you become more aware of how to put your express your frustrations to the other person rather than just snapping. You will come to understand what it means when you have to choose your anger. Does expressing your frustration lead to productivity? Or does it harm? After this, you then make a better distinction between whether it was the circumstance that made the other person angry or if they were indeed mad themselves? This then determines how you would proceed.

Reminding Ourselves of Our Humanity

In an incident that happened later in his life, Aurelius was presiding over a court hearing that involved a volatile billionaire Herodes. In a moment of the exemplification of the consuming madness of rage, Herodes lunged at Aurelius but was stopped by a guard, who wanted to impale Herodes with his sword. But, Aurelius stopped him and adjourned the hearing. Throughout the incident, Aurelius remained calm and collected, not betraying any anger. As a lifelong student of Stoicism, Marcus Aurelius was able to maintain and indeed acknowledge the humanity of someone who seemed hell-bent on harming him.

This is one of the more significant teachings in his books, The Meditations. When we become angry, we tend to look at the other person out of the context of their humanity. Through distortion, we reduce the entire other person's existence into this one instance and, thus, see them then as objects that deserve to be punished because of failing us.

But it is this kind of problematic thinking that led to Seneca declaring that anger was a danger to humanity as it could easily be infected from one person to another. This behavior is typified through 'mob psychology.' To make people come together and work as one cohesive until often takes resources and management, yet, it seemed to be that anger got people cooperating quicker. This was because led on by the desire for destruction, people quickly reached into their basal instincts and acted upon that as since it is easier to let yourself get carried away by your primal urges, it is easier than for anger to let us devalue another person and thus, act in a manner contrary to what we collectively share as human beings, our collective conscious.

Seneca called on us to heal rather than punish those that wrong us. Aurelius asks us to look at ourselves in the eyes of the person that angers us, or that hurts us.

Through seeking to correct the other person rather than punish them, we will then act in a manner that views and acknowledges their humanity and, therefore, the truth that they are prone to make errors and that the incident with you is but one of the mistakes.

Look back at when you were angry at someone. Did they seem to stop mattering? What mattered to you in that state of anger was that they had wronged you, and they needed to pay. This then meant that you overlooked the reality that they may have abused you because they didn't know better, or that the people were also dealing with issues of their own that they did not know how to handle it. We come across such people throughout our lives. People that do wrong without the knowledge that they are doing wrong.

Pausing to understand that they could be ignorant of what is widely considered right or wrong could go a long way to making you deal with how they act towards you. Again, this doesn't mean that you excuse bad behavior. Instead, you become more aware of how other people's actions shouldn't affect how you react.

Removing Ourselves from The Competition

Social comparison, as psychologists call it, is a form of state of being where measure our progress by looking at how others in a similar situation are doing.

This comparison is advantageous to us for a variety of reasons. For one, by looking at where others are, we understand better where we are and where we are going. It also offers us a peek into what qualities we would want from the other person and incorporate that into our own. This is what has driven us to build the things we have.

Through social comparison, then, we get competitiveness. In a bid to be better than the other, we become driven by the desire to stay ahead consistently. However, competitiveness has a side effect – anger.

Imagine the number of times that sportspeople have come to blows when the tensions run high. Imagine the anger that seethes in you when your friend, who supports another team, goads you when their favorite team wins more trophies and beats your favorite team.

When taken to the extreme, called compulsive competition, this anger at competition may result in a person becoming livid even when there is no apparent reason to be. Because of the nature of competitiveness, everything becomes a competition, meaning that anger is always lurking.

To manage your anger, take yourself out of the competition and instead aim for a more tranquil mind. Aurelius calls on us to eschew things beyond our control that make us angry. These things include competition. You will never be ahead of everyone, and this realization is what we should then use to guide us in working on our anger.

In one of his most important teaching, Aurelius called on us to work together, following the Stoic principle that saw us all as kins, and thus, we worked better through cooperation rather than through conflict, which results from competition taken to its extreme.

Putting this to practice is something that, indeed, can and will be challenging. Throughout our lives, we have known competition as the way to exist. But you should turn your mind to the law of abundance, which states that there is enough for all of us. Rather than view another human being as a threat, we view them as another team player, eager to build humanity like the rest of us. Making ourselves our competition then means that we will guide our actions based on what we can control, rather than putting faith in outward forces that we cannot control and whose happening is widely erratic and unjust.

Fulfilling Our Roles towards Others

This view that we are here to exist in harmony is a significant part of Stoicism. Throughout his book, Aurelius spoke of our obligation towards our fellow human beings, suggesting that 'we were born for something other than this' about our anger at our fellow human beings.

Socrates called on us to fight the urge to repay evil with evil and wrong with wrong. There was nothing right in doing wrong.

When we look at the text of Stoicism, we begin to understand that, through calling on people that adhere to it to get more in touch with who they are, the philosophy is calling on us to become better human beings by understanding our failings and our strengths.

The four virtues of Stoicism all call for us to fulfill what will, in turn, be of value to the other person. Through an insistence that we focus more on events that we can control and not on external factors and circumstances, we will be able to understand ourselves better and what we stand for.

It is indeed unfortunate that many of us claim to be standing for justice or truth or morality but then turn out not to be espousing the virtues to their core. This is not based on the nature of humanity to error. When someone claims to be moral and asks others to be virtuous, but then act consistently in a manner that is not in contradiction with what they claim, then it is not a case of human error but rather, a failure by the person to properly understand what the value entails.

We see this all the time. Someone claims one thing in public, but then it turns out that they are doing the exact opposite in private. When caught out in the double lives, the claim is always that they errored. But to espouse the virtues of Stoicism, one needs to be well aware of who they are and if indeed they do value their thoughts concerning other human beings. To become selfless, you will need to understand the depths of your selfishness. To then become a just, moral, and person of courage, you need to understand how you have perpetuated injustice. You will have to come to terms with your moral failings.

When you can be more forgiving to yourself of your failing, then you will also extend this forgiveness to others when they fail. You become better at teaching what you value.

When you don't espouse these values, but make a claim to uphold them, what will happen then is that to prove how deeply you value them, you will be punitive to people that err genuinely in their journey to become better. You do this to calm your guilt about not upholding these values. You do this to make those that esteem these virtues applaud you, which is why the loudest moralists turn out to be scam bags. The purists turn out to be nothing more than loudmouths. The people that claim to be may turn out not to understand how justice functions.

Thus, as an obligation to the people around you, and humanity in general, become more in touch with your person. Understand who you are, your emotions and feelings, your beliefs, and actions. Know then, that you can do better and make the effort of doing better. To fulfill your role better to others, then, means to fulfill your role better to your being.

Chapter 13: Stoic Philosophy and Anger

Stoicism calls for us to examine ourselves and use that to make the world around us a better place.

Thus, anger was one of the main issues that Stoics faced and attempted to dissuade us from falling into, as it is the beginning of the fall from a virtuous existence. It's not hard to see why? Almost every one of the stoics virtues, courage, wisdom, morality, and moderation, fall apart when you get angry.

Because of this, the Stoic Philosophy has a few lessons for us concerning anger.

Anger is Madness

At least temporarily, at least. Seneca calls on us to avoid it, as, even when it is justified to be angry, acting out of anger still never results in a positive outcome. He stated that, while every other emotion affects our judgment, passion went on and disrupted out the state of mind. It made as insane for the duration of the anger. A look at social media sites will indeed offer you a glimpse into the madness that is anger. People write and print all things that they would otherwise have not done had they taken a moment or two to deal with the exploding feelings.

So, to become angry was to go mad. To manage this, then needed to take a pause and question our anger. Chances are, it was unnecessary.

Anger Makes Things Worse

Marcus Aurelius stated that the effects of rage were bound to be more than the circumstances that led to it. When you get worked up at your friend for breaking your phone, that would only worsen the friendship and cost you your friend. Getting mad at another person will only result in a broken relationship between the two of you. Getting angry at an inanimate object will work you up for nothing.

In all these instances, anger works against you in every way at the end. Your character suffers, as you then become someone that people will want to avoid. When you argue with another person, it then means that they have a reason not wish to associate with you. Anger lingers on long after you have presumably expressed it. It is what led to Seneca to see it as something that, once gets a hold of someone, it became difficult to wrest back control.

To Deal With Anger, We Need to Acknowledge Humanity

The view by Socrates that no person ever does out to commit wrong willingly ruffles a few feathers, but it is crucial in helping us deal with anger.

Through the lived experience, Stoicism encourages us to take a moment when angry to see how the other person may have a life beyond the state in which they exist in that particular time – the state of 'this person made me angry.' When you look at the person as a whole rather than the parts, you then become able to understand their actions and, thus, why you should not allow yourself to become angry.

Thus, you then shift your focus from seeking to punish this other person, an action that would make you angry, towards telling them how their works of anger are harming them. You become more compassionate.

Chapter 14: Stoicism Reveals Rituals That Will Make You Confident

Probably, you have read hundreds of articles either online or elsewhere, about how to make yourself happy, become confident with yourself by exorcising negativity from your life, and boost your self-esteem so that you can live happily with yourself and everyone else around you. Yet, you are still stack in negativity, and you have not become a thousand times happier. So, you find yourself confused and begin to curse yourself for investing your time reading stuff that doesn't work. You are not alone!

There is a fundamental difference between reading stuff and putting what you have learned into practice. You don't expect to read good books on cooking and then become the best chef in the world! You must put that knowledge into practice, and invest hours of experimenting with it so that at the end of the day, you emerge victorious as a result of the knowledge you gained from the books. You will never kick like Bruce Lee by merely reading martial arts books. You must go out there to train and practice your behavior, to make the necessary changes and adjustments.

That is why the stoics, the ancient masters of wisdom, didn't write stuff for mere reading. They went a step further and created rituals and exercises that had to be performed daily to train the mind to respond positively to life events so that one can live well and happily. They warn us of the danger of getting satisfied with the mere reading, without practice and training, because with time, we forget what we had learned and begin to do things the other way.

Today it is fascinating to see modern scientists agreeing with what these ancient masters of wisdom used to talk about many centuries ago. We can't help then but to turn our mental eye back and look into what these gentlemen suggested may years before we were born.

Things happen in everyday life that make us feel like we are not good enough. When we make a mistake, or when something unpleasant happens to us, we find our brain making a replay of every other failure and mistake we have ever made. Just like that, our self-confidence gets crushed, and our self-esteem dips. This is an old problem, and as long as there have been people in the world, they have gone through such experiences. It is an ancient problem with ancient solutions. Ancient stoicism comes to our aid during such times. They realized that unless we learn and practice to question irrational thought and unhealthy beliefs that crush our happiness, we cannot perceive ourselves or the world clearly for a better, fulfilling life.

They understood that our feelings emanate from our thoughts. But the question is, "How do we get rid of our irrational and unhelpful thought that crush us, and allow rational and helpful thought to reign in our minds." Here is how we can use stoicism rituals to achieve that.

Identifying and Challenge Distorted Thoughts

This ritual is about learning how to monitor the voice in our head. That voice in our head passes harsh judgment to us when we are down. Let's say that you have engaged in a particular project, and then it fails. The initial thoughts that come with such experience are usually irrational and unhelpful. The voice in your head begins to condemn you for having wasted your resources, making futile attempts and makes you think that you are a complete failure. Due to such thoughts, you begin to feel down, unconfident, and uncomfortable with your abilities.

The Stoics knew that identifying such thoughts was an important step. When your self-esteem dips or when you are gripped by a feeling of lacking confidence in yourself, what is the voice in your head telling you? This is a way of getting beyond the feeling and looking into what is causing such a feeling. The aim is to identify the thought system, which is behind it. So you need to be able to follow your thinking process and capture the thoughts which are pinning you down by generating feelings of worthlessness.

For example, "I felt sad because I thought I was a failure." Or "I felt unworthy because I thought I was used up and taken for granted." Identifying such thoughts is vital so that you can move to the next step of challenging them. Capture thought like:

- I'm a complete failure
- I'm stupid and foolish
- I'm an idiot
- I will never amount to anything
- I will never get a job
- I'm ugly and disproportional in shape

These are initial thoughts which come in your mind when life events crush you down. The stoics suggest you identify such condemning and distorted thoughts and challenge them. But how do you test them? After identifying these thoughts, here is how you can challenge them: for every distorted thinking, provide a rational thought to replace it. Look at several examples below:

- **Distorted:** "I have invested a lot of my time and effort, but finally, I have not achieved anything. This project has been a sham, and I wish that I had not started it!

    Rational: "Even though I have not achieved what I had intended, I have learned a lot through my mistakes. I will learn from my mistakes so that I will not repeat them in the future. I'm a young man with a lot of potentials."

- **Distorted:** "I will never get a job. I lack the courage to stand before the interviewers, and any time I do, I shake uncontrollably. I'm doomed to fail."

    Rational: "I will have to do something to master my confidence during interviews. I will practice in front of the mirror and practice public speaking in small social meetings before my next interview."

- **Distorted:** "I'm not beautiful. My shape looks awful in the mirror. Any time I get into a relationship, I get dumped within two months. I'm awful, and nobody loves me."

    Rational: "I need to take control of my weight and get back to shape. I have ignored my weight loss program for two years now. I'm great and beautiful, but I have to make some little adjustments."

Test Your "Core Beliefs"

This is about the beliefs you have about yourself. Sometimes, these chronic feelings of lacking confidence and having a poor image of oneself go beyond negative thoughts. Lack of faith in oneself can be a direct result of having negative "core beliefs." There might be an inner critic inside you who presents consistent evidence to you about the kind of a loser or unlovable person you are. As a result, you come to believe that lie because you have not taken your time to challenge such belief by questions its validity. The stoics prescribe that we should make it our habit or ritual, to challenge or core beliefs.

Challenging your beliefs is not easy, given that such a fundamental idea may have already taken roots and are now forming the basis of every decision you make. Confronting that layer who wants to prove his case that you are a loser by always presenting concrete evidence in your head can be a daunting task.

The first thing that you need to do to deal with this lawyer who keeps on prosecuting you and condemning you to be a loser is to analyze the kind of evidence presented on your end. Write a list of proof as to why you feel that you are unworthy. It may sound funny, but this step is essential. The stoics suggest that you write down everything that makes you believe that you are a loser. You need to analyze and understand the evidence of this prosecution lawyer so that you can devise the best method to poke holes on it.

What you have been lacking is a defense lawyer on your side, to address the negativity confirmation bias that you have suffered. With your inner voice aggressively presenting evidence to you as a loser, you end up seeing things in your life that agree with the idea that you cannot amount to anything.

To counter that, the stoics argue that you should also make another list of evidence. This list acts as evidence that the lawyer prosecuting you from within is wrong. It should have all the reasons and ideas that prove that you are not a loser. This new list of evidence aims at altering the settings of your beliefs so that you stop noticing the unhealthy feelings and force you to look at all the things that have happened in your life to see the evidence that supports your healthy beliefs.

The stoics also suggests that you find a co-counsel. You need a friend or a family member or any other person you can trust, to remind you of what you are excellent in, by pointing out all the great things that you do. Getting such confirmation from someone you believe makes you feel valuable and important, and bring to the surface some crucial evidence that you may dismiss by seeing it be insignificant. Even if they see things like counting, that you don't think should count, put them on the list. This list of concrete reasons as to why you are valuable and impressive will help you to silence the prosecutor from within by replacing the biased evidence of negativity with the evidence that is rational, accurate, and honest.

Have an "Evening Confidence Ritual"

After digging deep and addressing your core beliefs, your inner critic will still attempt to linger on. The change will not come overnight. You need to keep on programming your mind so that you can fix all those false beliefs and prevent them from popping up again. The Stoics understood thoroughly the power of an evening confidence ritual in fixing negativity and keeping it at bay. They knew that by taking some time to reflect every day can bring tremendous improvement. It is an excellent way to watch over yourself by taking sometime in the evening to review your life.

After confronting your inner critic with all the reasons as to why you are not a loser but a winner, the battle continues. Reflect on your life by taking some time at night and think of all the things you are good in and what you have achieved that day, and come up with more evidence as to why you are not awful. Since now, you have become less reactive on yourself, accumulate a daily evidence log to enable you to develop healthier beliefs.

Reviews are essential, and they are common in business, especially annual reviews. The stoics knew the power of reviewing one's day to improve the quality of life. Sometimes you need to look back into your past to understand your future. Think of what you have done during the day and ask yourself whether it worked well for you. Reflection makes it possible for you to monitor your daily life by thinking of how the activities you have engaged yourself in have helped you to become better. Do not hide anything from yourself, or pass anything.

Reflect on what you did right and the thing you didn't get right that day. Reflect on the things that you were supposed to do, but you dint do them. Such knowledge is vital as you plan on how to improve your tomorrow. Don't condemn yourself for the things you didn't do or the one you didn't wrong. Learn from your mistakes and forgive yourself. Having self-compassion and forgiving yourself is what prevents you from repeating mistakes as well as avoiding further procrastination.

Don't beat yourself up or be critical of your abilities. Capitalize on the thing you did well during the day, and use them as a basis for doing better tomorrow. Appreciate yourself for the good things of that day, and continue doing them tomorrow. It is a great way to extend your blessings. Promise yourself that you will not repeat the mistakes of today tomorrow, without being critical or judgmental. This is a master key to self- improvement, and happiness. As time goes by, your positive belief will become prevalent, and the inner critic will begin to go silent.

Use a "Cognitive Cue Card"

At this point, you have identified and challenged your thoughts, dug deep, and scraped your negative beliefs, and you are making an awesome follow up by taking an evening review of your daily life. But there is one more step if you are to realize stoic self-confidence. You need a cognitive cue card to help you monitor further the negative chatter so that you don't give in to it. A cue card acts as a quick reminder, and it contains frequently used information, such as reminders and prompts.

Sometimes when you are distressed, you need a quick response to wipe out such distress within a moment's notice. You need a way of challenging that inner critic any time no matter where you are. You need a way to make such a challenge smoother, instead of spending a lot of time arguing with yourself. This will help you avoid the back and forth that can make you look like an insane person.

There are those negative thoughts you are accustomed to, and you keep hearing them so often. That is where a cognitive cue card comes to your aid. You need to have a set of immediate responses to such thoughts so that you can counter them with positivity immediately they appear. Write such responses on your cognitive cue card so that you will not have any difficulty remembering them.

Sometimes you are tired of arguing with yourself. At such times you may notice that your mind is heading in the wrong direction. That is the best time for your cognitive cue card to come to your aid. Use it to counter the obvious negative thoughts and keep your interpretations rational.

In the heat of the moment, a three by five notecard comes to your aid in enabling you to keep doing better. It helps you to think differently during less-calm moments. So, during tranquil and less calm moments, writer down on your cognitive cue card the things you believe you would want to hear during stormy times when you are tired with less time to argue.

For example, when you face failure, you can have a cognitive cue on your card, which says, "Just because I have not achieved my goal, it doesn't mean that I'm a loser. By learning from my mistakes, I can achieve greatness." Carry your card with you and use it to learn to be self-compassionate. It is not going to be easy, but by repeatedly practicing to tell yourself sensible and rational stuff during awkward moments, you will finally master this stoic ritual.

Programming your mind with stoicism rituals will take time. Sometimes you will screw up, but consider that to be normal. Continue reprogramming yourself by taking small steps of practice every day until you realize your wellbeing. Don't be a perfectionist as no one feels 100% confident, but focus on progress as you continue to become better. You have a right to be confident.

Chapter 15: Stoic Philosophy Ancient Wisdom in the Modern World

Stoic philosophy is a different school of thought from other schools because it teaches practical wisdom. Its philosophy is anchored on actions. The belief of stoics is that application is the end, while debate and thought are just a means to that end. The stoics teaching of self-control, virtue, and tolerance has been a great source of inspiration to both thinkers and leaders for many centuries. They believe in four cardinal virtues which lead to happiness and fulfillment in life. These are courage, wisdom, temperance, and justice. Now the question is, we should practice these virtues in our modern world to live with confidence, fulfillment, and happiness.

Striving for improvement

Stoics believe that change is constant. A lot of change is happening in the world today, more than any other time in history. Yesterday's solutions may fail to work for today's problems. But these stoic principles are eternal. They work all the time. They can help us learn to change with the times and keep learning new things as the world changes. New knowledge will help us to see opportunities instead of whining about the challenges.

Face the world as it is

To face life with confidence, we should learn to meet the world as it is. Stoics believe that we should learn to appreciate the world as it is, instead of debating for years on how it should be. There is nothing wrong trying to think outside the box and bring changes, but that can only be done after we have first appreciated our world and accepted our place in it.

Don't worry about what is beyond your control

You are at the airport. The management announces that the next flight has been canceled because the weather is not conducive. You begin to yell at every airline worker you come across. What good will that do to you? You will only wear yourself down with unnecessary stress. Who is responsible for that? You have no control f over the weather. Stoics teach us to only worry about what is within our control and direct all our resources towards it. Worrying over what we can't control doesn't solve anything. This is important if we are to live happily in our modern world.

Keep a journal

In our modern world, we need self-reflection more than ever. We should learn to document our lives so that we can monitor our achievement by recording our ideas, plans, and goals. Taking time to reflect on our progress, achievements, success, and failures will help us have better ideas on how to live happily in our modern world, which is changing very fast. Stoics knew that, and that is why they advise us to reflect on our daily activities each time before going to sleep.

Chapter 16: The Four Cardinal Virtues

Cardinal virtues are the essential moral qualities that a person needs in order to lead an upright life. A person with cardinal virtues acts right in all aspects of their life because they have high self-control. The virtues are also in line with the scripture.

Wisdom

It is also called prudence virtue. It is said to be the mother or source of all the other virtues that follow. This is the first virtue because, as the name suggests, it deals with human understanding and intelligence. This virtue involves a person understanding the right things to do and actually doing them. By the use of this virtue, all human beings have the ability to tell what the right thing to do is and the wrong thing not to do. When someone chooses wrong over right, they are just ignoring the wisdom virtue. However, this does not mean condemnation for people who do wrong, as sometimes the mistakes are genuine. It, therefore, calls for seeking other's opinions and advises before making decisions on things you are unsure of. Some people are very good at telling them right from wrong, and those are the people that should be sort for help. When you ignore your prudence and others, you are merely imprudent. One cannot practice the other virtues when they lack prudence because they have no wisdom to determine and follow through. Wisdom will show someone the effects of doing something and the consequences of not following through things.

Justice

This is the second cardinal virtue, and it comes second because it is all about a person's will power. The willpower to do what is right to ourselves and also to others. To give another person what is rightfully theirs, we need to have the willpower to do that. Otherwise, one may be aware of how to do right but does not do it because they lack the willpower to exercise justice. When doing the right things to others or exercising justice on others, nothing should stop us. It does not matter how much we dislike the person or how much below our class they are, what is rightfully theirs should be accorded to them. If someone became your enemy after they had given you money, as a person exercising justice, you should pay them back. This is because the enmity has nothing to do with the justice you are, according to them. Justice is positively giving someone what they deserve, no matter how helpless the other person is. When someone is denied justice, it is called an injustice. The person has been denied what they deserve even when they have a legal right to it. Even when someone is not bound by the law to do what is right, the conscious will tell someone what is right. For this reason, even those who feel above the law should practice justice. This is because the natural instincts of justice are within each one of us.

Courage

This is also known as fortitude and is the third cardinal virtue. This virtue deals with the courage to conquer any sort of fear and be firm in our willpower. When we get rid of the fear, we are able to face any difficulties in life. However, having courage doesn't mean that a person should go looking for trouble to prove they are courageous. It merely means that when the danger comes after us, we have the willpower to face it instead of running away. Therefore, the virtues of wisdom and justice give us the ability to tell right and wrong and how to exercise them. Courage gives us the strength and willpower to implement the two other virtues. Without courage, one has wisdom and knows what is right to do, but they lack the guts to actualize it. This is a gift of the Holy Spirit as Christians believe. Not everyone is gifted with courage. Courage will make a mighty man give respect to a very common man because they have the courage that helps them realize that it won't make them any weaker doing what is right.

Temperance

It is also called self-control or moderation virtue. It strengthens courage virtue. This is because courage helps do anything without fear. However, without self-control, one may end up doing the wrong things thinking as a showoff of courage. It helps a person put aside their own personal desires when there is a greater reason to help others. If a person does not have temperance, they do not care about others, they will only do what is right for them, and it is usually selfish. Temperance gives us the ability to balance things out. Yes, our needs are essential, but if having these needs will be harmful to others, temperance restrains us. It is also through temperance that we are able to deny ourselves of 'too much' on things because too much may be harmful. Temperance sets the limits for us; without this virtue, there are no boundaries on things that we do. It helps a person say stop when they have had enough of something, and it is time to stop. For example, food is good and an essential means for our survival, but when we overeat (binge eating), it becomes harmful. If someone were to have anything they wanted without self-control, there would be a lot of destruction. There would be a lot of immorality in society if people ignored the virtue of temperance. It also means that people can use drugs; however, they want because they do not control themselves. Without self-control, people would steal and kill as they please. It is therefore very important than no matter how powerful a person is, they practice temperance.

The four are, however, are not the only virtues, but all the others that come after are somehow connected to the four. However, without even adding other virtues, the practice of these helps people co-exist with respect and peace. It is essential that everyone learned to practice these virtues because, from this, all other virtues will be easy to follow.

Chapter 17: Incorporation of Stoic Philosophy into Everyday Life

Stoicism is the ability to let go of things and situations that are not in our control. Most times, we want things to go as we plan them to, and when they don't, we get frustrated. Stoicism helps us let go of this burden of letting go of things we cannot control. Stoicism gives hope at our most desperate times, right before we sink into depression for worrying about things beyond us. As human beings, we are always trying to make things our way, and this gives us anxiety for overthinking things. The best remedy for fighting this is practicing stoicism no matter how difficult and depressing the situation is. Ignoring stoicism will only cause someone pain because, in the end, if it is beyond you, there is nothing you can do about it.

How to Practice Stoicism

The most important thing is to realize the things and situations that you can control and know what is not. When you know what is beyond you, it helps you not to waste too much energy on something beyond you. Knowing that something is beyond prepares you for any results and therefore enables you to avoid unnecessary stress. You help your mind realize that the outcome might not be favorable, and therefore you are able to deal with any issue. When you do not establish what is beyond you, your mind goes through a lot of stress because it feels like one is merely weak. Each person needs to know that everyone has something beyond them, no matter how strong, powerful, or wealthy they are. Changing our perspectives on things we cannot control protects us from damages that would result from constantly worrying.

We should learn to work on improving ourselves. Knowing what our limits are is good, but it does not mean we relax or lose hope. Some things are beyond us, but there is always something we can improve on what we cannot control. Learning to grow in different areas is a stoic principle because it encourages us to keep practicing instead of giving up. However, improvement does not mean perfecting. We cannot perfect something beyond us, but we can improve on that thing if we do not give up but instead keep practicing.

An example of this would be given in a classroom set up. A student may be very poor in mathematics, and they have done the best they can, including private classes for the same. Stoicism dictates, instead of focusing on it and being depressed because it can lead to failure in the other subjects, the student should work on improvement. This does not mean that they work to be the best in math class, just that they should not quit trying, especially in a compulsory class. The practice may take them from a poor percentage to a better one that counts a lot.

We should also strive to live our lives exactly the way life happens for us. This means finding something to be grateful for in every situation. Sometimes life will be unfair, but instead of stressing about this, we should take every opportunity to learn from it. Accepting that we cannot always get what we want gives us inner peace. Stoicism also means that we accept people in our lives and try to co-exist. You cannot change people; we all have different feelings, thinking, and ideas. We should be able to accept each other exactly as they are. Trying to change people will only hurt you as a person. A person can only be changed by themselves. However, if we change our attitudes towards how we react towards people, we do not agree with, this is stoicism.

Taking action instead of giving up is a stoicism practice. Stoicism means you let go of things beyond you, but it does not mean you sit back and relax. It does not mean that you quit taking risks and start feeling sorry for yourself. Things don't just fall into place; we work hard to get things to happen. You cannot control the situation, but you can manage your actions by using different strategies. Maybe things are not working out because you always do them in the same way over and over again. Change the strategy; you might not get the exact result you hoped for, but you will achieve an outcome, good or bad. It is an outcome that should be a lesson for you. Accepting you have no control is not enough, you have to go and try to get things done but in line with the moral values. You do not want to try to compete with something beyond you and end up in trouble. So this means that whatever you are seeking is in line with the cardinal values so that you are protected.

Practicing stoicism also means that we discern right and wrong and making sure to do what is right. This means practicing the four cardinal virtues, which are prudence, justice, courage, and temperance. When you practice doing what is correct, it means you are able to give value to everything around you. People want to be rich; no one ever wants to be poor. Stoicism comes in that you live right. You do not have to steal from people so that you become rich. A stoic person will work hard and let riches come to them naturally. However, someone who does not practice stoicism will take the action of stealing, corruption, and all the bad virtues to acquire wealth. How you react towards any given situation determines how much stoicism you practice. A stoic person always tries to follow the virtues and let things flow as they should, but the opposite person takes power in their hands and tries to do all the controlling.

Take prevention measures for anything that could go wrong. You cannot control your body from ever falling sick, but there are some diseases that you can prevent yourself from. Take preventive vaccines for those diseases. This is called the prevention of misfortunes. Prevention of misfortunes means always having your mind prepared for any disaster that may befall you. Being ready helps a person be in control of their emotions in events they cannot control. It means that you are prepared to surrender to the events but very in control of happiness. Being ready for misfortunes means that any bad results will not determine your joy because you have already accepted the consequences beforehand. When you are mentally prepared that anything can happen, you then make plans for a plan B or even C. It means you have not placed all your eggs in one basket because you well know they could all break. Being ready for misfortune does not mean we are anticipating for bad things to happen. It only means we are ignoring the likelihood of things going wrong. The reason people are so overwhelmed by circumstances in life is that they are caught by surprise. Not being in control of circumstances does not mean we cannot protect ourselves from any harm that may befall us.

Stoicism also encourages that you keep a record of all your day's happenings. A journal is essential because it acts as a reminder of things we are likely to forget. We make decisions in our minds to do something or change something. However, it is very easy to forget things only if we think about them. Writing about things we intend to work on, we help us keep check of ourselves. A journal also helps someone look at their progress from where they started to where they are right now. A journal enables you to get the pattern of how you do things. You could be thinking something is beyond you because you keep failing. Then using the journal, you realize that you have been using the same strategy all the time. A journal will, therefore, help you note places you can work change on. You can change your plans very fast even before the end results because of a pattern an alert you on time. When on the road to improve on something, the journal gives us a routine. When you have established what to practice on, you need to keep working on it. A routine will help you not change your plans along the way before you have achieved your intended goal. We cannot fully trust ourselves to remember everything; each moment we learn something new, we always end up forgetting the old stuff. If something was recorded, however, it will be unforgettable because you can still read it through. A journal also helps us appreciate ourselves better. Instead of being too hard on ourselves, we can look at the journals and see things we achieved. Some things we achieved were once too difficult for us, but if we met those, then we are reminded we can achieve anything. Journaling, therefore, encourages someone to take risks they would never have considered.

But most importantly, journaling helps us know ourselves better. Not only does it help us realize where we fail, it helps us understand the strategies that work for us, and it also helps us see the very many obstacles we have overcome.

Chapter 18: Growing Up Stoic (Philosophical Education for Character, Persistence, and Grit)

Parents and guardians are encouraged to teach children about philosophy at home. This means teaching children how to handle any obstacles they are likely to face in life, as early as possible. For the parents to do this, they have to be aware of the real virtues which they are expected to pass to their children. Stoicism says that virtues are inborn; we are born with the ability to tell right from wrong. It is, however, up to the parents and guardians to ensure that kids do the right things. Our happiness and personal satisfaction are gotten when we do the right things in life and being of good character. When children are made to practice virtues, they eventually become good and can control themselves from making random mistakes and poor decisions in life.

It is not enough, though, for parents to teach their children and be strict with the children to do right. Parents and guardians must also practice what they preach. This means that they have to be a perfect example of what they teach. When a child is told to do something, they are more likely to do it if they watch their parents do it. This is not to put pressure on the parents to be perfect; it merely means being real with your child. Let your child know that you are also wrong sometimes, but you always strive to be right. Let them learn how to move past the several mistakes that they make in life by being an example. Teaching the child can be derived from the following virtues.

Justice

This means teaching your child to be just and fair in all their doings. Therefore, a child should be taught to be kind to others. When they are kind, they will feel for others when others are in pain and need help. When a child is just, it means that they are able to put their interests aside to help others. Children who are not taught this are very selfish and do not care about the pain they implicate on other kids. A child who is just trying to protect others who are not being treated fairly and that they do their best to be fair on others. The child is even willing to go out of their way to make others happy by helping when needed. Only a child who has been taught justice can do all this.

He Goes On to Say

In this, a parent is encouraged to create ways of making the child more charitable and able to say no to things. Some kids usually get everything they have and do not realize that other needy children do not even have the basics. Teach your child that that thing they are crying for is not as important as they think, and they can do without it. Teach your child to forego luxuries and help the more disadvantaged kids. This can only be encouraged by exposing kids to situations they have never experienced. Let them go and see the homeless kids and see how they survive. The chances are that the child will say no luxury the next time and ask that the money be used to help the homeless children they saw. In short, this means letting a child have a say in kind gestures because they already know that there are more deserving people out there. The child should be encouraged to help out more than asking for things they may not need.

Determination

Virtue encourages parents to help their children get determination, which is basically giving a child the courage to do things. This can be achieved by allowing the kids to help out in chores at home when they are still young. By helping out, children are getting life skills like courage, determination, and confidence to do various things. When they are helping out, they learn about hard work and why determination is essential to keep pushing on. They get the fulfillment after they are done helping out, which is the result of the determination.

Moderation

This virtue involves teaching children how to be moderate in doing things. Controlling their emotions, controlling their eating, and managing everything literally before it becomes too much and harmful for them. Just like adults, children also have felt they need to know how to handle. It is, therefore, important to sit your child down and talk to them about their tantrums. Let them know that it is alright for them to be angry, but it is also essential that they control it. Teaching a child to be moderate in their decisions involves letting them assess their situations. Ask them if they think their tantrums were worth it, and if they believe there is a better way, they would have communicated their frustrations. This will help a child see for themselves how they would have been moderate in their emotions. In eating, kids do not understand why they have to eat certain foods. They want to eat only sweet things. They should be taught why moderation is good at eating. Why it is essential for them to eat healthily and why it is essential not to overeat of whatever they want to eat.

Wisdom

This virtue helps a child know right and wrong, have the proper judgment on things, and accept the things beyond their control. A parent can help the child by sitting with their child every day in the evening and together analyzing the child's day. Let the child say the things they think they did right and the things they feel they did wrong. Help the child know what they would have done differently so that the next time they are in a similar situation, they can make better decisions. Encourage the child if they are feeling helpless for things they had no control over. In doing this, you are instilling wisdom in your child. A child will be able to make better decisions in the future and even be able to let go of things beyond their control.

Conclusion

Stoicism is very important in society; it can be attributed to being the reason why the world is peaceful. It is due to stoicism that people are able to co-exist. Stoicism is very fundamental for every single person whenever we are facing hard times. During hard times, stoicism gives us the hope to wake up, dust ourselves off, and press on. We are taught to let go off of the things we're unable to control. Without stoicism, we would all sink into depression because we all go through hard times. Nations would fight each other because there is no control, and a country can go after another as they please. But because we have stoicism, we have globalization. Nations with different people of different cultures and colors care and help each other. That is why nations will send relief food to nations that are going through war or drought. Stoicism is also the reason why nations will accept refugees into their countries.

It is through stoicism we learn that our failures do not define us. Therefore, instead of worrying that we failed, we try different strategies. We learn through stoicism that we all have weaknesses but that we have the ability to move past our shortcomings if we practice stoicism. We learn to be real with ourselves, to forgive ourselves for things we did wrong.

Our leaders are able to deliver for the people only if they practice stoicism. This means that they put the people's interests before their own. The reason why we have increased corruption, injustice at the courts, and increased immorality is because leaders do not practice stoicism. As rational human beings, we are able to live peacefully with our neighbors despite them being too different from us. We accept them with all their flaws and look past them because we understand that we cannot change them. It is also through stoicism that we are able to keep ourselves from judging people when they do things we do not agree with. Letting them do whatever they want as long as it is not hurting us.

It is through stoicism that there are courts of laws. This is to help people who feel they are being treated unjustly to get the justice they deserve. The lawbreakers are also imprisoned to help correct them because society wishes the best for them. Without punishing the criminals, then the courts are not being fair to the victims.

Stoicism helps us appreciate life. We stop looking at situations and feeling sorry for ourselves when things are not working out. Through stoicism, we are able to appreciate the little we have and the ability we have as individuals. Being grateful for everything, no matter how life makes us love life and look forward to brighter days. As humans, we learn to have empathy for others, and we also get the wisdom to help us in life. Stoicism is, therefore, very important and should be practiced by every person in society. We can only be able to understand each other as human beings if we are all willing and determined to practice stoicism.

Finally, if you found this book useful in any way, an honest review is always appreciated!

www.ingramcontent.com/pod-product-compliance
Lightning Source LLC
Chambersburg PA
CBHW060408080526
44583CB00012B/507